PRAY Ye

HE THAT PROMISED IS FAITHFUL

Silvia Lia Leigh

Then Jesus told his disciples a parable to show them that they should always pray and not give up.

~Luke 18:1

DEDICATION

To my Lord and Savior Jesus Christ, this book is for your glory.

To my husband and co-laborer in the vineyard of the Lord, thank you for your support and assistance.

CONTENTS

PREFACE

Prayer has a life of its own. No one can teach me prayer if I refuse to pray. It is not just theory, not just a Bible study or doctrine. It is my life with my Father and my own identity in Him. I should accept the fact that if I stop to pray, that would be sin and suicide. Prayer is a fruit out of real communion with God. I cannot learn how to pray successfully, and at the same time refuse to live like Jesus or be disobedient to His Word. God cannot be manipulated. Conditions have to be fulfilled before rewards are given. This is a spiritual law that none can break.

Just like the study of the Word, prayer is like eating food and drinking water. It has to be done daily, if not, we shall become spiritually weak. If you call yourself a believer and you do not have a daily appetite to study God's word and pray, then you should be very worried about your standing with God.

I shall depend totally on the leading of the Holy Spirit as we embark on this journey to unwrap the gift of prayer. My aim is to give glory to God, and to be conformed into the image of His son Jesus Christ, our Lord.

The meaning of the word 'prayer' in the simplest form is man talking with God. There are many religions in this world and all prescribe prayer. I shall limit myself to the prayer of the Christian, as we see it in the Bible.

We cannot overestimate the importance of prayer. If we say that we are believers, then prayer is basic; it is the language of infants. A baby coming into this world that makes no sound at all is dead. He may be beautiful, have two arms, two legs, even a head and a mouth, but if there is no sound at all, then there is the silence of death.

Finally, prayer is comfort. Each prayer reminds me that I belong to someone, to a family, and that I can never be alone. Each prayer is an exchange of whispers of love and kisses of trust that take me out from this ordinary life into the Spirit that knows no end. During prayer, I stretch my wings of faith to fly, to touch the rainbow of peace above the dark clouds of the storm. I see the door open, I hear the future sing, I dance to the melody of strings in heaven and I embrace the Amen. This is my prayer!

ACKNOWLEDGEMENTS

Pasturing at Father's House Bible Church continues to be a rewarding service, I owe special thanks to all that have encouraged me to be a women of God. It is because of your love and support that I am able to write this book to the glory of God:

To all the members of Father's House Bible Church, I am warmed by your faith, may God bless you!

To the Women's Fellowship in our church, because of your commitment to the word of God, the Spirit has allowed me to pen love letters from my heart to yours. It was these letters that were priceless in refining the message of this book. May God bless you!

To Matthew Oakes, my hope when you started working on the cover was for our hearts to align in the spirit in the image and message of *Pray Ye*. Thank you for being so receptive and letting God use you to speak my heart.

To Veronica Kuyinu and Jemine Leigh Oakes, I want to say how much I treasure and appreciate the time and effort that you spent editing the pages of this book and your personal encouragement and help will always be remembered; I am grateful. May God bless you!

INTRODUCTION

There are many books written about prayer. This is a good thing because prayer and the study of the Word of God are vital for the maturity of the believer. The purpose of studying the subject of prayer for me was the fact that I wanted to discover revelations, to challenge myself to a higher level of faith when I pray to God. I already knew that prayer 'works.' I did not want to take for granted the blessings received in the past.

What I re-discovered in the Word of God is that prayer is the most powerful force in the universe, especially when it is done in an attitude of worship. Men and devils may stop material blessings to come to me, but no one can stop my heart and my mouth to pray. This discovery alone is enough for me to continue to remain in an attitude of prayer until my last breath. I love the freedom prayer gives me, far from the burden and boredom of the routine of daily life. In prayer I discovered that no one can replace God in my heart, because no one but God is able to listen to me for so long and in all circumstances of life.

I was born in Romania almost sixty years ago. I grew up in a loving family of four. My parents were teachers in the school which I attended with my younger sister, Adica. We did not go to church at all. The only contact I had with religion was at Christmas when the priest of the church in town would come to visit people and wish them happy holidays. He would come dressed in a long black dress, ringing a little bell in his hand accompanied by his younger assistant. My father warned us to run inside when we saw them, because, as teachers, they were not allowed to invite religious people inside the home. I remember how afraid I was of the priest's black dress, his bell, and his mysterious chant.

Sometimes, my father would 'feel sorry' for the priest, as he was ringing the bell outside the door, standing in the heavy snow. He would quickly make a gift of homemade bread, salami, cake, and wine. Then my father would go outside, after switching off the front light, he would give the gift to the priest. Only the stars were witness to their meeting. All we heard behind the door were many words of gratitude and blessings 'in the name of Isus' (Jesus). Adica and I thought it was funny. I thought that my father was very bold to go outside and embrace the strange looking man. Stranger still was the feeling left behind that Isus sent him to greet us at Christmas. We would never remember the visit or the words until next year again at Christmas.

Many years passed before my father told me that he was once in the seminary with the desire to be a priest. But the communist take-over after the war closed down almost all bible schools and changed them into colleges of education. My father was forced to choose, and this is how he had to let go of his dream to serve God, and instead became a history teacher. The priest that came every Christmas to our door was one of my father's colleagues at the seminary. He was one of the very few who chose to continue with his calling in ministry and he eventually became a priest. Life separated them, and the cold winter Christmas Eve, was the only time when they could give a quick hug with many painful apologies from one, and a flood of blessings from another. That was all that I knew about God and His servants until I came to Nigeria.

While in medical school in Romania I met my husband Richmond, a Nigerian. After graduation, we moved to Nigeria to start a practice in 1980. We became successful as medical practitioners. We had money, fame, and everything man could desire. What else could one possibly want? Nothing! Or so I thought.

As I write these words, my heart worships and sings. For more than thirty years as an atheist, I knew of no god that could answer prayers. I thought that religion, with all its practices, was just like medication for unhappy people. I used to say that I would rather take anti-depressants prescribed by a doctor, than to deceive myself by praying to an invisible God. I was living in a world of doubt and unbelief and I had accepted the lies instead of truth. I did not have to review my stand because I was not challenged enough, I did not see any effect of prayer in the lives of religious people. All this changed when I met some true believers who did not just pray, but rejoiced in their faith and boasted about knowing their God. They had no fear of death. They challenged me to try prayer. I remembered that I was shocked by their boldness and assurance.

My stronghold of doubt started shaking. Though I refused to pray with them, I found myself secretly longing for a personal God who cared for me. The very idea that there is a God who 'has time' for me, who wants to listen to me, patiently waiting for me to unburden my soul, that idea was for me 'too good to be true.' But then I started asking myself:

"what if this God is true?" I remember saying that religious people have an expanded imagination; that they live in a fantasy world and their ideas couldn't be real. I was amazed when suddenly I heard a voice in my heart asking me gently but confidently: "what if God is real?" This voice indeed surprised me. I did not know its source. I did not know its purpose. I did not know if it will last for more than a moment. But the voice challenged me to think about spiritual things, about eternal things; the very things that I denied for so long. Wrapped in the cloak of false humility, I considered eternal things to be the domain of the proud and foolish. But the question still lingered… 'What if God exists?' I remember feeling 'trapped' by the voice. In the past I could force myself to forget anything I counted as unpleasant, anything that tried to shake my long preserved 'peace of mind.' This question about God had a double effect on me. The first feeling was that of fear, like standing face to face with one clearly stronger than me. I tried my old skill: to forget, to ignore, to deny the question. This method always worked in the past. I became skilled at avoiding 'bad' things. But this time, my strategy failed. For whatever reason, I could not forget or deny the truth. Simply said, if God exists and He is looking at me at this very moment, if He indeed is calling my name, then… 'I am …finished!'

I remembered feeling lost and ashamed. In January of 1986 I became very depressed. I saw nothing good in my achievements. I lost my desire to live. In the midst of my despair, for the very first time in my life, I prayed.

Pray Ye

CHAPTER ONE

LORD, TEACH US TO PRAY

GOD'S COMMAND

One day, Jesus was praying in a certain place. When he finished, one of his disciples said to him: "Lord, teach us to pray, just as John taught his disciples"

~Luke 11: 1

We see in the scripture above that the disciples were impressed with the prayer life of Jesus. They did not really ask Him for many things; they did not ask Jesus to teach them how to preach, but they asked Him to teach them how to pray.

Let us stop here to ask ourselves a few simple questions: do you have a desire in your heart to pray to God? Do you pray from the internal impulse of the Holy Spirit or just because men force you to pray? Think of it! The truth is that the child of God has a built –in system in his heart that makes him happy to talk to God, anytime, anywhere. The desire has to be there, no man can give it to you. But we still need to know 'how' to pray, the royal, priestly protocol of addressing God in such a way that He will acknowledge our prayer.

The meaning of the word 'prayer' in the simplest form is man talking with God. Some of the more familiar definitions of prayer are:

- PETITION: humble, earnest request to God – asking for an answer, information, a revelation, help, or a favor from God;
- FELLOWSHIP: communion with God – a family meeting between children and their Father;
- PRAISE and WORSHIP: to express profound admiration, to honor God;
- CONFESSION: to plead to God for forgiveness of sins, cleansing and restoration;
- THANKSGIVING: to give thanks to God;

- INTERCESSION: to plead for others, to persuade to a course of action;
- LOVE MANIFESTED: a love letter from friends and lovers of God to God.

In Hebrew, the word prayer has more than one translation. Generally it means to judge a matter mentally or officially, and based on that, to petition God. It means to intercede for others; to praise and worship God. Lastly, it means to give thanks to God.

In Greek, the word prayer means to express a wish, an earnest desire to God, to vow to God and to praise and worship Him.

Pray continually… Be unceasing in prayer- praying perseveringly (1 Thessalonians 5:17; NIV, AMP). Jesus was a man of prayer. He was God living in human flesh on earth. He was always in communion with the Father. He was an obedient Son. He did not decide anything alone except through prayer, in union with His Father. This is a very important spiritual principal that we should never forget. If you desire to be like Jesus, then you have to believe that prayer is the lifestyle for the believer.

Prayer is a privilege. Jesus lived and died to teach us how to pray and to give the access, 'the password,' the key to the Father's attention and presence. If Jesus did not pray as a Man, we should have had no business to pray, no matter what any religion says. But the truth is that Jesus Christ prayed continually.

Looking at the scripture above, what do we understand by it? We are commanded to pray continually, without ceasing and with perseverance. Why is it so? Is it because the Father did not hear us when we prayed the first time? The answer is No! The Father hears all His children who call on Him. In fact He hears our faintest whisper and our heart desire, even before we call. Then why pray so often and so long? It is because our flesh and our hearts are deceitful. During the long time of standing on prayer, God communes with our spirit. In my experience, God will allow His child to come with a particular request into His presence and then He 'changes the subject.' Let me say that suddenly I forget my initial request and little by little I get excited about another project my Father is telling me about. At the end of it all, it looks like I went in with a particular burden and I came out with another one. It has happened to me many times. I think this is because God allows us to come before Him with any request at all, but He alone is the One that knows the timing and the sequence of the events and blessings in our life. I have also learned that prayer is coming into the presence of the Father, and the anointing changes me, my motives and desires. I find myself praying for the same topic, for instance; the salvation of my children, but after being in His presence, I see it differently. Same God, same prayer, but a different me!

Just like the study of the Word, prayer is like eating food and drinking water. It has to be done daily, if not we shall be weak spiritually. If you call yourself a believer and you do not have a daily appetite to study God's Word and pray, you should be very worried about your standing with God. Examine yourselves to see whether you are in the faith; test yourselves (2 Corinthians 13:5).

Prayer is a very accurate way to test your spiritual state: if you are born again or not, Spirit filled or not. There is always a danger that you are just a religious person and not really saved or you are backsliding already. The flesh hates prayer in private. It does not mind prayer in public to attract attention upon itself, but hates to pray when there is no audience to impress men. It has been said by many, and I found this to be true, that in church, the least attended activity is the prayer meeting. People like to come to sit and listen to a preacher or to the choir singing. As long as the flesh can 'rest' in the chair and be passive, man does not mind to come to church. But prayer means to be active, body, soul, and spirit. Prayer humbles you; it is work. Prayer makes you 'sweat' in your spirit. There is something about a prayer meeting that you can't just come and 'relax' or 'enjoy' when others pray. You have to make a choice, to join in the spiritual labor or leave. Occasionally, I see people struggling 'to meet up' with the request for prayer, but after some time, they get tired of the labor and fall back into passivity. That is why we are commanded to pray 'always.' It means to keep the fire of the spirit burning, if the flesh likes it or not. It is hard for the true believer and it is impossible for the fake. Prayer discriminates and that is why the flesh hates it.

The prophet Samuel, when confronted with the rebellion of a whole nation, said something that should be an encouragement to all of us who chose to pray: As for me, far be it from me that I should sin against the Lord by failing to pray for you. And I will teach you the way that is good and right (1 Samuel 12:23). In Hebrew, the word 'failing' means to cease, to become idle and unoccupied, to rest from, to abandon, resign and forsake my duty before God. We are to pray during times of success and during times of sorrow. The circumstances around should not influence

5

my emotions to the extent that I abandon my position as a watchman who prays. Men are prone to sin, to be disobedient. This is a fact. We should not allow the sin of others around us to influence our spiritual life. This is a great warning, especially to the leaders. Moses failed to enter the Promised Land because of his unguarded reaction to the rebellion of the people. This is a very sober warning.

Let's test again the level of commitment and persistence in prayer. If our conscience condemns us about this wonderful work of God, may we ask Him for forgiveness, cleansing, and restoration! God's commands are not difficult of burdensome for His children; they are in fact a joyful proof of their love for the Father (1John 5:3). "He gives us more grace when the burdens grow greater…" says an old song. So true!

O, the joy to be found in the presence of the Father when bringing petitions and intercessions and waiting for an answer, any answer! The reward to such a special labor is nothing less than God Himself. God's house, the church, should be a prayer filled place. I will give them joy in my house of prayer (Isaiah 56:7).

Who needs the joy of Jesus? Who is tired of depression in this world? Come to Jesus and let's join Him in a family prayer meeting to the Father! That is the safest place in the whole universe! Come and pray and see that the Lord is good!

Let's pray:

Dear Heavenly Father, I thank you for the privilege of coming into your presence to pray. Forgive me for neglecting the time of prayer. Restore me back to the blessed place of joy in your house of prayer. In Jesus' name I pray. Amen!

CHAPTER TWO

THE PRIMARY DANGER TO PRAYER

HYPOCRISY

"And when you pray, do not be like the hypocrites, for they love to pray standing in the synagogues and on the street corners to be seen by men. I tell you the truth they have received their reward in full"
~Matthew 6: 5

Let us look at what the Lord has to say in the Sermon of the Mount about prayer. In chapter six we see how Jesus describes the right and wrong way to do good deeds, to pray, and to fast. There is something common in all these. We are told that the primary danger in our religious life is hypocrisy. Let's look closer at the meaning of this word and be ready to repent of this sin. It is the cancer of the believer's testimony. Because our heart is so deceitful, we need radical treatment so that we can be free.

A hypocrite is:

- An actor; he plays the act of a religious man to gain an audience
- A double life man: believes one thing and says (preaches) or does another thing
- A deceiver: bad heart and good 'face' (good manners); gives false impression
- A self-righteous man: judgmental, easy on himself, but strict on others
- A false man: not genuine, not faithful, he lies and misleads others intentionally, so that they will fall

The hypocrite that Jesus is talking about is not born again! He is a religious fake man; a religious unbeliever. He loves the church atmosphere, but hates Christ. It is like a man who loves a married woman and wishes the death of her husband so he can marry her. A hypocrite is a man who loves to come to church and to do ministry. He is not lazy, but zealous to do activities that people see as noble and good. He is often known as a 'prayer warrior.' His desire for recognition propels him to be very active in the church.

The hypocrite loves the fame that comes from being seen as a man of prayer, a spiritual man. He is attracted by the call of prayer done in public. He does not have 'a quiet time' with God if there is no one around. His secret desire is to gain popularity among religious and non-religious men. We are told that they pray 'standing' inside the synagogue or the church to impress religious men. They want to attract anyone passing by when they pray 'on the street corners.' The word 'standing' in Greek means to be appointed, established, and confirmed in a permanent place of ministry. He gives the impression of 'a mature leader.'

The hypocrite prays with great passion and many words but the hidden reason is always the same: he wants 'to be seen by men' and recognized as great. When praying, he gives the false impression that he is intimate with God. His prayer is a performance intended to amaze and attract followers. Never underestimate an 'old' hypocrite. He has mastered his trade; 'a professional' who has gained experience and he knows the weakness of his victims. Like flies into the spider's web, many have fallen into his net.

What exactly does a man like this desire? The best answer is given by the Lord: they work very hard so to gain the praise of men. They want to be famous. "How can you believe if you accept praise from one another, yet make no effort to obtain the praise that comes from the only God?" (John 5:44)

I read somewhere that 30 percent of all adults daydream regularly that one day they will be famous. This rate is higher among teenagers. What is the definition of fame? It means to be a celebrity, to be widely known, and easily recognized wherever you go. Many are attracted by famous people and are ready to obey and even worship them. It is the desire to become a 'god.' It is this pride of life that is the root of hypocrisy. The devil was once 'famous' in heaven as the worship 'leader' of the angelic choir. His fame was not enough for him and he became jealous of God, who was his Creator. That became sin and he was thrown away from heaven. The devil now is the most infamous creature in the whole universe. His bad reputation as a liar and the father of all lies can never be erased. He is the source of all selfish ambitions, jealousies, deceptions, fake believers, false prophets, and hypocrites in church and outside church.

Deception is not an isolated example. The world is made of hypocrites and they have perfected their own trade: who will deceive who? Some are better than others. Some are masters, champions, mentors, and others are students and followers. But the name of the game is deception. Religion is a very attractive field for the hypocrites. Sinners do not want to be known as wicked, ungodly people. Most of them desire religious fame and friends in the churches. They know that prayer is a standard requirement for a position of leadership in the church. So they learn how to pray well until others come and openly admire them.

GOD LOOKS AT THE HEART, MOTIVES, AND PURPOSE OF ACTIONS

King Saul was a head taller than the rest. His height was part of his credentials to be accepted as a king. Most people like what they see and hear; natural gifts are highly prized by men. Beauty, height, good singing voice, diction, confidence, gentle manners, the talent to dress well... all these gifts are investments of gold in the treasure of the world. Prophet Samuel was sure that Saul would be king in Israel. But later, when he had to make a second choice, he made the common mistake of choosing a leader based on appearance. He pointed out David's senior brothers as potential kings. Thank God for his correction, if not, David the greatest king of Israel would not even be mentioned in the Bible. "Do not consider his appearance or his height, for I have rejected him. The Lord does not look at things man looks at. Man looks at the outward appearance, but the Lord looks at the heart" (1Samuel 16:7). The word 'looks' in Hebrew means to consider, to experience, to approve, to respect and enjoy. Here we see the vast difference between the thoughts of God and of men; so far apart, like the heavens and the earth (Isaiah 55:8, 9). The heavens is not only far from earth but much greater in size and glory. This is a very important spiritual principle: God looks at the heart, the secret place, the interior motives and spirit. "All a man's ways seem innocent to him, but the motives are weighed by the Lord" (Proverbs 16:2). "Surely you desire truth in the inner parts; you teach me wisdom in the inmost place" (Psalm 51:6).

If men will simply believe these scriptures, they will never fall into the trap of hypocrisy because they will know that none can deceive God. The hypocrites attract others like them who are less skillful in the game of deception or baby Christians, who have not yet learned their utter dependency on God. That is why we are commanded to look for the spiritual fruit in the lives of religious men and not be impressed with gifts alone.

What is the cure for 'the yeast of hypocrisy' when it comes to our prayer life? It is to repent of it in the name of Jesus who exposed it as sin. We have to prove our repentance by developing a secret, intimate, quiet walk with God, for the sake, honor, and glory of God alone. We are commanded to go into the inner room, far from the eyes of men. We should not fear men but we should be careful that we don't attract attention upon ourselves as being overly spiritual people.

There is a desire I have: that people should not see or remember me, my face or my person, especially when doing ministry and under anointing. When I have to lead a prayer meeting, or when I preach the Word of God, I imagine myself hidden behind the cross of Christ. The cross is my address on earth. If anyone sees me, he should see Christ crucified first of all, and me through the filter of His sacrifice. Sometimes I hear people complaining to one another; "you have forgotten me," I make every effort not to say that. In fact, I pray that people forget me and remember Christ alone.

As an unbeliever, I used to be afraid of being rejected or ignored. I highly appreciated the few friends I had who always remembered me, my jokes, and my gifts. Looking back, now I see that much of that was a game of praising and flattering one another. The flesh indeed profits nothing. I lost all my worldly friends and now I am more satisfied with Christ and what He provides for me in this world. When I pray to Him, the eyes of the people admiring me are a snare to my soul. Why would I like to be seen? Why do I need an audience; when I can talk to the Lover of my soul?

I heard someone say that 'Prayer is done for the audience of one.' I like that! God alone hears me, my words, my sighs, and my tears. When I make mistakes in speech, God never corrects me because He knows what is in my heart and He also knows my weaknesses. Thank God for tongues! I don't have to impress God, He knows me too well. I also don't have to impress men, because it profits nothing. In the past I thought that pleasing God is hard and pleasing people is easy. I discovered that the truth is quite opposite. This revelation came slowly as a reward to me, especially during the times of prayer. The more I prayed, the more I understood God as my Father in heaven, strong and gentle, patient and kind, like no man can ever be to me. Yes, prayer has rewarded me with the knowledge of God. That is why prayer for me can never be a mere religious routine for as long as I live. Yes! I love to pray to my Father in heaven!

Looking back, I see how much I have changed. I was an atheist for over thirty years; I did not believe in prayer. Now I teach others about prayer! God is wonderful!!!

BAD FRIENDS DESTROY YOUR PRAYER LIFE

Hypocrisy is more common in the church than you can imagine. Hypocritical friends have a destructive power; their presence around you will injure both your prayer life and your testimony as a believer.

Jesus said that all church people are divided onto two groups: the sheep and the goats. There is no middle ground. The sheep are true children of God. Many have weaknesses; some may lie or pretend for a season, but they will eventually repent. No true child of God rejoices or continues indefinitely in unrepentant sin. On the other hand, all goats are hypocrites. They come to church, sing, dance, worship, pray, and give offerings... but they are not truly saved the reason why we study them is because we are warned not to be deceived by them. They are agents of the devil planted to deceive believers. We are warned to be careful with people we call friends. Friendship with hypocrites is dangerous because sin is infectious. We learn to imitate that which is close to us. The choice of friends reveals a lot about the condition of your heart.

We are warned not to pray like the hypocrites. But staying close to them, joining the same prayer meetings with them, will affect the way we see prayer and our relationship with God. Remember that the hypocrites are not true believers. They do not pray to God the Father. They pray to their imagination of God, to a mental idol really. They know no spiritual protocol, no fear, and no attitude of worship in Spirit and in truth. Do not underestimate the danger of pollution to your heart coming from the religious hypocrites. "A righteous man is cautious in friendship, but the way of the wicked leads them astray. Do not be misled: Bad company corrupts good character. Come back to your senses as you ought and stop sinning; for there are some who are ignorant of God- I say this to your shame. Do not share in the sins of others; keep yourself pure" (Proverbs 12:26; 1 Corinthians 15:33, 34; 1 Timothy 5:22).

Hypocrites are called 'bad company.' This unequal yoking destroys the good reputation and the Christian testimony among the brethren. Hypocrites are false friends. They lead you away from Christ; they will discourage you to repent from sin. Through gossip and wicked counsel they will lead you astray into more sin, away from God and His grace. The primary intent of the devil through his agents is to deceive the believer into a false security and the foolishness of pride; these open the gate of backsliding. First, it brings shame to the name of Christ and secondly, to you and your family. We are commanded to awake to righteousness (1 Corinthians 15:34; KJV).

The word 'awake' in Greek means to rouse out of sleep, from stupor; to be sober, to not be drunk with wine, to watch, to be discreet, and to abstain from all things that inflame the emotions. It means that friendship with hypocrites causes an artificial joy, a stupid happiness that leads to irresponsible behavior, like a drunkard. A man in stupor is dull, foolish, careless, slow, lazy and passive. With a mind that is so dull, surely, his prayer life is affected. This is because you need to be alert and sensitive to the leading of the Holy Spirit, to discern danger ahead and be watchful as you pray. These things are all connected. You have to choose between bad friends and serving God! No compromise allowed!

CHAPTER THREE

BE WATCHFUL

GOD WARNS AGAINST CARELESSNESS

"Two women will be grinding grain together; one will be taken and the other left."

~Luke 17:35

Imagine two women, both working together, talking about different things. Jesus said that they sit at the hand mill and grind, to produce flour from grains. Their work is hard and boring. It is almost like punishment. Remember Samson, the enemy punished him by removing his eyes and forcing him to grind in prison. This monotonous job leads to foolishness and depression. There is nothing interesting about a job like this.

The women look the same from the outside, but God looks at the heart. We are told that suddenly there is a separation: one is taken and one is left. Jesus is talking here about the rapture, in particular. But we can apply the warning to life in general. The word 'taken' is a friendly and loving word. It really means that when Jesus calls you by name, you will be ready to respond instantly, with amazement, surprise and worship. What makes the difference between these two women? It is the heart! One is a child of God, praying, worshiping and faithfully waiting on God. The other woman is just a 'co-worker,' possibly in the ministry. God looks at the heart and the final destination is written there. Apart from rapture, promotions happen suddenly to a child of God. The 'co-worker' has a hopeless future; nothing to look for, no one to intervene and change the boredom of daily grinding. This is a simple question; is your heart praying through the daily routine of life? Can you worship God in the most difficult circumstances, even without the encouragement of others around you? If the answer is yes, then you are blessed because you are a God's child.

Therefore keep watch, because you do not know the day or the hour (Matthew 23:13). A similar picture is the story of the ten virgins in Matthew 25. The two groups of women look so much alike. All are virgins, young and beautiful. But beneath the beautiful faces the hearts are different. The wise ones are children of God. They pray, worship, and prepare for an encounter with the Bridegroom. They purchased their lamps and enough oil for the long wait. The foolish ones brought just the lamps, trying to imitate the wise ones. This is the typical behavior of religious people, the hypocrites in the church. They clearly did not have a relationship with God, no quiet time, no prayer life, and no worship. That is why they did not recognize the need and the value of the oil, which represents the Holy Spirit. They ignored the trial of long waiting and just fell asleep. Consequently, they were denied entry into the wedding feast. That is the judgment upon the foolishness of hypocrisy. It always ends in disappointment and closed doors.

"Watch and pray so that you will not fall into temptation…" says the Lord (Matthew 26:41). Bad friends weaken the capacity to wait, watch, and to stand in faith. Therefore they will weaken and eventually destroy your prayer life. It is the Holy Spirit that gives the power to stand and watch for danger. To do warfare in particular, you have 'to stand' (Ephesians 6:13). This is a great responsibility for all believers and especially for the wives as we pray for our homes.

'A prudent wife is from the Lord' (Proverbs 19:14). The word 'prudent' means to be discreet; to have the wisdom and strength to watch and detect danger and attacks against the marriage and family. A similar word is to be discreet, meaning to show good judgment in speech; to be able to keep a prudent silence. Prudence and discretion in a woman are sure signs that she is born again and filled with the Holy Spirit.

Now let us look at two women of God, Esther and Abigail, who showed godly wisdom and prudence, especially in times of danger. May these two sisters be an example of spiritual maturity for us! We find both their stories in the Bible; the book of Esther and the book of first Samuel verse 25. Both married kings and were wise, humble, and beautiful. Both had difficult marriages, they had to submit to hard men. Both met the danger of death and had to quickly find a solution to it before it was too late. We see that they were spiritual women of prayer and intercession. Esther and Abigail knew the royal protocol; when to talk and when to keep quiet, when to be visible and when to remain hidden. Their words were filled with truth and grace that none could contradict or resist. They had faith that God could change an impossible situation into victory.

It is clear that these two women had wisdom from God on how to intercede. Their hearts were prepared through prayer and fasting. This is the real source of boldness to confront kings when they are in error and that saved the lives of many. This type of wisdom comes from dwelling in the presence of God, far from the eyes of men. Long time in prayer and worship will change your heart and prepare you to confront the crisis that will decide your destiny (Proverbs 21:31). It is not clearly written but we can easily deduce that both Esther and Abigail were women of prayer. Their boldness to act in time of danger is the proof that they knew how to 'approach the throne of grace with confidence so that we may receive mercy and find grace to help us in our time of need' (Hebrews 4:16). We can also assume that they abstained themselves from bad company that corrupts the reputation and the testimony of a woman of God. It is clear that Esther could not make friends with somebody like Mrs. Zeresh Haman. Abigail surely could not come close to Nabal's drunken friends or their wives. God blessed both women with a small inner circle of loyal and trusted servants who kept them informed about things outside and were ready to serve them always.

Both women were rewarded with great and unique blessings. For saving her people, Queen Esther became a hero to all the Jews who still celebrate the festival of Purim and remember her. Abigail's reward was marriage to King David, by whom she had a son, Kilcab. It looks like she had no son with her late husband. Both David and Nabal were from the tribe of Judah. It is possible that David married her as a Kinsman Redeemer, just like Boaz married Ruth. Kileab was not seen in the struggle for power for the throne in Zion. He and his mother possibly went back to inherit the great estate of Nabal. 'A sinner's wealth is stored up for the righteous' (Proverbs 13:22). This is a beautiful picture of the story of redemption, the defeat of the devil and the glory of God seen in the Gospel of Christ. This is great reward indeed!

Finally, each one of us should test our hearts and the foundation of our salvation. Bring to the Altar of God all your friendships and let them pass through the fire of God. The hypocrites may be entertaining to many in the church, but be warned: they live under the wrath of God! "The sinners in Zion are afraid; fearfulness has seized the hypocrites: Who among us shall dwell with the devouring fire?" (Isaiah 33:14, NKJ). You don't want to be found in the company of the enemies of God, the religious hypocrites. God forbid!

Let's pray:

Dear Heavenly Father, we come to you to ask for mercy and grace in the time of need. We ask for forgiveness for the sin of making friends with the children of darkness, with religious hypocrites. We ask for cleansing by the Blood of Jesus. Help us to be true and faithful to you alone. We trust you to bring new and good friends to us. We love you Father, in Jesus' name we pray. Amen!

CHAPTER FOUR

ALONE WITH GOD

PRIVATE PRAYER

"Do not be like the hypocrites... But when you pray, go into your (most) private room, and closing the door, pray to your father, who is in secret; and your father who sees in secret, will reward you in the open"
~Matthew 6: 6; AMP

In the above scripture we are told that private prayer is to be done in a special place, 'behind closed doors.' The Lord Jesus commands us to go and find that hidden place, even before we open our mouths to pray. It means that prayer starts with a preparation, a searching for the acceptable altar. This seeking requires faith in God and it is the fruit of love for Him who rewards this intimate longing for private communion (Hebrews 11:6).

Jesus commands us to go to our own room and close our own door. The address of this place is known by just two people: God and you. In this place, three are called a crowd. To have the key, means that you are the owner of the house or the child of the owner. It means that prayer acceptable to God comes only from His children. They alone have the key to 'the room' of access into the presence of their Father. 'Now a slave has no permanent place in the family (in the house), but a son belongs to it forever' (John 8:35).

Where is this place? First of all we can say that it is not a natural place. It is not a room in a house. It is true that it helps to look for a quiet place to pray. Jesus went often to the wilderness or lonely spots to pray (Luke 5:16). He called His disciples to do the same. The people around, with their needs and voices, are a distraction to a man praying. Learn to be jealous with your time of fellowship with the Lord. Selah!

'Jesus said to them, come with me by yourselves to a quiet place and get some rest. So they went away by themselves in a boat to a solitary place...' (Mark 6:31, 32). But even so, we are not called to find a physical

17

place to be with Jesus. Worship and prayer are now done 'in Spirit and in Truth' (John 4:23). This place of intimacy is a spiritual place of the heart, the holy of holies of my spirit. It is hidden from the eyes of men. It can be found only in the true child of God. The religious hypocrite knows nothing about prayer in the secret chamber of the spirit. He has no idea that a place like this exists. The hypocrite does not prepare his heart nor seek the presence of God before prayer or worship. The religious man is totally ignorant of any royal protocol. All he is interested in is the performance, the speech, the accent, and the content of his prayer. He does not address it to any one in particular. It is like he prays to himself, from his own imagination. The act of prayer discriminates and separates people. Jesus said that you are with Him or you are against Him (Luke 11:23). The prayer of the unbeliever is not just ignored by God but it is offensive to Him. All prayers are not acceptable to God! Selah! "The Lord detest the sacrifice of the wicked, but the prayer of the upright pleases him" (Proverbs 15:8).

NOAH'S ARK

"By faith Noah, when warned about things not yet seen, in holy fear built an ark to save his family. By faith he condemned the world..." (Hebrews 11:7).

The story of Noah is found in the Book of Genesis chapters 6 to 9. Let's look at Noah's desire 'to walk with God.' The word 'walk' in Hebrew means behavior that is the result of a holy habit of dwelling in God's presence. It is an established character based on long time obedience to God's voice. This type of man is conversant with God's ways and not only His deeds. The word 'walk' also means to grow in grace, to manifest fruit of the Spirit. It means to always move forward and to never look back; to flow, to travel with 'the cloud of God's presence' and to ignore all distractions to do otherwise. For a man who walks with God, prayer and worship is his air to breathe. That is why we are told that in his life journey, Noah found favor with God.

Noah was commanded by God: 'Make yourself an ark' (Genesis 6:14). The word 'make' is very powerful. It means to start a journey of activity, to be busy without rest until the project ends. It means to serve, to sacrifice, and to be a warrior ready to defend this labor of love until the purpose for which it was built is fulfilled. Noah obeyed God and by faith built the ark. It was a house on water that would save his immediate family and many animals. Noah had faith which 'condemned the world,' a world that was not interested in trusting or obeying God for salvation. There is another 'fearful' scripture that confirms all these. It defines an unbeliever as someone who goes to church, but is not interested in the provision of life, spiritual or natural, for his own immediate family (1Timothy 5:8).

The ark was designed to have a high window, next to the roof. The word 'window' in Hebrew is very interesting. It means a place of (double) light, a place for the olive oil to come in. In other words, the only communication with the outside world will be through the filter of the Holy Spirit. The eyes are 'windows.' When we pray we close them so that we only see with spiritual eyes.

The ark had only one 'door' on the side. The word 'side' in Hebrew is also very interesting. It means a secret, vulnerable place that needs total protection from the enemy. The door was so strategic, so important, that only God could shut it or open it (Genesis 7:16; 8:16).

This is a very important point to make. Prayer is not a series of unconnected, scattered episodes of talking to God. In prayer, you go into the presence of God and shut the world away. It is a dwelling, an uninterrupted abiding, a lifestyle, a walk with God that radically changes a man's character.

God creates Light. God separates Light from Darkness. This is His way always. In Noah's time we see that God applies the same principle. God separates the people into two groups: the righteous and the wicked. Noah and his immediate family are counted as righteous. They alone were saved from judgment and death. All the rest were destroyed by the flood.

The world is said to be interested in marriage and having children; the women are beautiful and the men are strong and famous. This is what is seen on the surface, but God says that He was grieved by the evil thoughts and imaginations of these people, by their evil, wicked and unrepentant hearts. They purposely ignore, resist and grieve the Holy Spirit. They are corrupt and love violence. 'Corruption' in Hebrew means to spoil, to waste, to lose, to damage, and to oppress and rape one another. The whole picture is one of total hopelessness and evil.

On the other hand, Noah finds favor with God, a man of prayer and a preacher of righteousness (2 Peter 2:5). The word 'just' in Hebrew means to be accepted, to be right with God. The word 'perfect' means to be a man of truth, to have pure motives, honest and good. God promised Noah that He would make a covenant with him to save him and his family from death. That salvation would be through the means of the ark that had only one door. Noah's preaching was fruitless, or so it seems. But here we are, reading the story so that the fear of God may move us to repentance.

The function of the ark was to save lives. All its content was safe from judgment and death. Please see this: the door separates life and death. Eight human beings and selected animals came to the ark for salvation. God said that they 'will come to you to be kept alive' (Genesis 6:20). The word 'kept' means to save, to guard and protect against the enemy. The word 'alive' means revival, to recover and restore, to nourish life, to be made whole. The flood killed all life outside the door. Noah stayed inside for exactly one year and seventeen days, not more, not less. That is a long time! Inside the ark it was not comfortable, like a cage with so many animals. But at the fullness of time God said 'Come out of the ark, you and your wife and your sons and their wives' (Genesis 8:16). They entered as eight different people; they came out as a family!

The world mocked and laughed. The clear distinction here between Noah and the world is a very useful picture to understand the warning of Jesus that we should separate from hypocrites. During the flood, how many of Noah's neighbors called his name, or tried to open the door? Jesus is the ark. Jesus is the door. 'What he opens no one can shut; and what he shuts no one can open' (Revelations 3:7).

I hope you see that the ark represents the secret place of pray and worship; the lonely, most private place in your heart where you commune with God. It takes many years to build it through much persecution and warfare. But O… the assurance of salvation, the security of the believer found only in the sweet hour of prayer and worship that no man can give and no man can take away. 'Go, my people, enter your rooms and shut your doors behind you; hide yourselves for a little while… until his wrath has passed by' (Isaiah 26:20).

'Come my lover… let us go early to the vineyards… there I will give you my love. The mandrakes send out their fragrance, and at our door is every delicacy, both new and old, that I have stored up for you, my lover' (Songs of Songs 7:10-13). Do you know the secret place where you can go 'early' to be one with the Lover of your soul? Is prayer time sweet to you? Have you stored beautiful things for Him who is never late to meet with you? Do you know Jesus? Do you know His glory, His power, His Spirit and His Word? Then you are saved and blessed indeed!

CHAPTER FIVE

TOGETHER WITH GOD

CONGREGATIONAL PRAYER

"When they heard this, they raised their voices together in prayer to God... After they prayed the place where they were meeting was shaken. And they were all filled with the Holy Spirit and spoke the word of God boldly.' 'So Peter was kept in prison, but the church was earnestly praying for him."

~Acts 4: 24, 31: 12: 5

In the previous chapter we studied private prayer done in the secret place alone with God. Let us now look at congregational prayer. The Book of Acts is the story of how the church laid the foundation to practically apply the teaching of the Lord. They were a small group of believers at the beginning, but they had mighty possessions: the authority to use the name of Jesus Christ, the power of the Holy Spirit and the Word of God confirmed by the apostles. We see here how the church gathers to pray, to have home fellowships, to study the Word, to execute discipline upon the rebellious.

Persecution started against the disciples of Jesus, many were martyred, but nothing could kill the Church because it was not just a natural gathering of people. The Church is the Body of Christ, the supernatural coming together by the Holy Spirit of people who are born again. You need to have a clear revelation of the doctrine of the Church as a Living Body, intimately connected with the Lord. The believers knew that 'Christ loved the church and gave himself up for her to make her holy' (Ephesians 5:25, 26).

As you study the prayers done by the disciples in the early days of the church, you have to believe that they were conscious of this love connection that none could destroy. That is the way they prayed with faith and with power. That is why God answered their prayers. Oh... that we may discover their secret and do the same!

21

These are four points that can help us to pray better as a congregation:

1.   Prayer is addressed to God!

This sounds so simple but the truth is that many believers are too distracted to pray well. Prayer is not talking to other people or to circumstances. Prayer is communion with God in heaven. Often we forget who the Person is that we address our petitions to. Simply said: we forget God! The problems we carry, the anxiety of the moment, the flesh that is weak and full of doubts… there are many factors why we pray 'amiss' for lack of focus. Jesus taught His disciples to start all prayers calling the name of God, 'our Father who is in heaven'. This means that preparation of our hearts before prayer is very important. Make it a holy habit to wait a little in the presence of God before talking to Him. It calms down your spirit and you become more sensitive to the voice of God who is never in a hurry. I still remember the great impact of the revelation on my soul in knowing that God is never in a hurry. All my friends, including myself, live in a degree of anxiety when it comes to the unknown. It is not so with God. He never frets, He never panics and He is never surprised at what we do. That is the God we serve forever.

As you wait in the presence of God remember that He is all powerful and all knowing. What seems to be a great problem is nothing before God. The secret to answered prayer is to be like God. When Jesus prayed to the Father, all prayers were answered. Jesus never experienced this doubt about the power, the willingness, or the love of God to answer prayer. We are to have the mind of Christ. During worship, you are to be on 'your side' looking at God and bowing to Him. During prayer you have to learn the secret to be on 'God's side.' Some people can't transition between worship and prayers. We have to practice both and it becomes easier with time.

2.   Prayer is to be done with faith and passion!

The second simple step in prayer is to have faith that God hears us when we pray in the name of Jesus. Again, this is such a simple revelation that many ignore. As you talk to God remember that you are before His throne of grace. You do not merit any blessing from God, not even the answer to your prayer. That is the truth. God does not deal with us from the position of merit. All God's blessings to men come because of the mercy and grace released at the Cross. That is the source of all the power of prayer. As you stand before the throne you will see 'the Lamb who was slain.' It is because of Jesus that we have access into the presence of God to pray. No other name or power is given to man on earth to approach God. The more you understand the Cross, the power of the Blood, the greater your faith and confidence during prayer will be.

We saw that the disciples prayed with all their heart, with passion and with earnestness. Prayer is never a 'casual' exercise. I am not saying that you should be a hypocrite to dramatize prayer acts. I am saying that if you trust the leading of the Holy Spirit, your heart will be challenged 'to feel' the things you pray about. At the end you will know that you have prayed! There is a type of tiredness that follows successful prayer which is a sign that virtue has gone out of you and God has been contacted. The tiredness is mixed with peace and quiet joy. The deal is done!

Do not be ashamed of your emotions. Some churches are so cold that it seems strange to pray with passion. My advice is to go away and look for another that allows the holy feelings stirred by the Spirit; it is as simple as that!

3.   Prayer is to be done in the unity of the Spirit!

In congregational prayer everyone must 'flow' as one. Ideally it is a prayer done by believers who attend the same fellowship. They have a common bond of believing the doctrines of the Bible. They understand that the Holy Spirit is in charge and they gladly submit to His leading. The spiritual agreement is true submission to God and to one another 'out of reverence of Christ.' If there are secret sins in their midst, the Holy Spirit will be grieved and will not 'move.' Pray for repentance before proceeding to other issues.

There is an unspeakable feel of being one with the Head and with one another. We are commanded not to forsake the assembly of the saints (Hebrews 10:25). We are to joyfully expect an encounter with the King when we gather to pray and worship as a local church. The experience is different than when you pray alone. God seems bigger and stronger. Of course God is the same, but the feeling is different and it helps your faith grow. The prayer agreement is a special type of prayer of the church. It requires at least two people (Matthew 18:19, 20). Both are believers, if not, spiritual agreement is impossible. It is not just a physical nearness. The believers have to trust the Holy Spirit to align their wills to be in one accord spiritually. Their faith will be 'used' to bring about this agreement before talking about other things in prayer. Of course it is easier with the more mature believers who have learned to die to self and be alive to God alone.

Marriage is a strong environment where the prayer of agreement can be practiced with amazing results. If you are married and you have not practiced all these things, your marriage is still immature and unsatisfying.

4.   Prayer is done until there is a 'shaking'!

I had to ask God for the boldness to add this lesson to the ones above. In the Book of Acts we see that prayer done by church was always powerful, followed by signs, wonders, miracles, and 'shakings.' That should be our pattern. We should never pray religious 'half- prayers.' The word 'shaking' means that God comes down in answer to the prayers of His people. Things change immediately. Nothing and nobody will be the same again. The fear of God is the most important feeling in the congregation once the Holy Spirit 'moves.' No man can make God perform. It is all by grace and mercy alone. During 'the holy shaking' the proud are humbled and the humble lifted up. This change of spiritual position is done immediately during prayer. The results may take some time to manifest, but what God has done is always final. The most important thing to remember is that God 'acts' on behalf of His people who pray. God may choose to be quiet for a long time, but 'He never sleeps or slumbers.' He gave us ears, so God hears. He gave us hands to work, so God performs and shakes all things for His glory.

Let's pray:

Dear Heavenly Father, help us to pray so the anointing of the Holy Spirit will flow freely through us as a congregation and the power of coming together as a church will manifest and enrich our prayer life. In Jesus' name we pray. Amen!

CHAPTER SIX

GOD LISTENS

THE SHAKING

*"I will make the heavens tremble and the earth will shake from its place
at the wrath of the Lord Almighty, in the day of his burning anger."*
~Isaiah 13: 13

Let us look in detail at the effect of prayer done in faith and in the unity
of the Spirit. There has to be a shaking! The word 'shaking' means to
move to and fro, to vibrate or to agitate. It also means to frighten, to dis-
turb, to intimidate. To look at this word from another perspective, it
means to become free by destroying the bondages. For example, to shake
off a sickness means to be healed, to revive and to gain strength. To shake
off an organization means to re-structure and to re- arrange, by destroying
the former connections and positions in the offices.

Spiritually speaking, God's shaking destroys created, temporary,
thing of the flesh. It weakens and destroys the enemy, the devil and his
works of sin. It destroys all yokes of bondage, the false foundations and
the effect of the religious spirits. The effect of shaking is freedom for the
captives and revival. The eternal things of the Spirit can never be destroyed by any shaking. The effect of shaking is to see the difference
between the flesh and the Spirit, between religion and true Christianity.
It becomes very clear that this shaking is similar to the Baptism of fire
granted by the Lord Jesus. Once His eyes of fire look and touch any situation, there is an instant change that none can stop.

THE SHAKING AND THE FILLING WITH THE SPIRIT

"After they prayed the place where they were meeting was shaken. And
they were all filled with the Holy Spirit and spoke the word of God
boldly" (Acts 4:31).

In Acts 4 we see 'a strange' answer. It looks strange but it should not be so. The truth is that God shakes and changes things and none can stop Him. The believers were in great need because of the persecution. They prayed together a desperate prayer that they should be strengthened against the threats of the opposition and to continue to preach boldly. Fear is an evil spirit and they needed deliverance from its grip and power. They asked God for the boldness of faith and anointing to preach the Word of God to be used as 'a hammer that destroys the rocks' (Jeremiah 23:29). They prayed and God answered with a shaking of visible and invisible things. Nothing was the same again. One of the effects of this shaking was that all hindrances against the filling with the Holy Spirit were removed. Doubt and fear were destroyed instantly and the Spirit had free access to their hearts. This was God's solution to their need. It is the same today! Be filled with the Holy Spirit! Power comes with the Holy Spirit! What a great revelation.

After this power came, you can see its effect; the unity of the Spirit and the grace increased upon the believers. In Acts 5 the enemy inside the church represented by Ananias and Sapphira was destroyed. We see healing, miracles, deliverance, supernatural strength to endure persecution and the power to rejoice in the sufferings of Christ, the church manifest a strange power to establish and increase the kingdom of God. Many were martyred but none could stop the church, as a body to prosper.

If you are praying for revival; the Book of Acts is the standard textbook. The subject of prayer and power should be our passion as we seek to mature in Christ. There are still many questions without answers, but we should press forward and pray for deeper revelation. 'Jesus is the same yesterday today and forever' (Hebrews 13:8). We should be encouraged to know that our God is the only Living God and He delights to answer the prayers of His children. The Church is the Body of Christ, and to belong to it is indeed the greatest privilege.

Do you understand these things? What does God's shaking mean to you? Have you experienced it personally?

THE UNSHAKABLE KINGDOM OF GOD

'At that time, his voice shook the earth, but now he has promised 'once more I will shake not only the earth but also the heavens.' The words 'once more' indicate the removing of what can be shaken- that is created things- so that what cannot be shaken may remain. Therefore since we are receiving a kingdom that cannot be shaken, let us be thankful and so worship God acceptably with reverence and awe' (Hebrews 12:26-28).

In the Book of Hebrews chapter 12 we see described two mountains, each a symbol of a kingdom. For a time, each one had its own 'tourist' attraction. For a time both look the same to us. Later we see that God's shaking is manifested and with one 'blow' He destroys one and establishes the other. Let's look closer at these mountains and kingdoms: The first one is a mountain of fire; noisy and fearful. Darkness and smoke cover it. It is the natural mountain called Sinai revealed in the Old Testament. It is the mountain of the law that makes no man perfect. It can be touched, but not carelessly. Death is all around it. God sounds angry and unfriendly. There are no words of comfort coming from Him, only warnings of punishment and death. There is loneliness and fear. Moses was able to go to the top only because of the grace of God extended to him alone. He had no fellowship with other brethren on this mountain. All the people ran away with no desire to listen to the voice that 'shakes' the mountain. This is the rejection of all flesh, even the religious one. God gave the law, but because of the weakness of the flesh, it could not be kept. At the foot of that mountain of fire, convicted by our own sins and the failure of the flesh, we finally bow down in surrender and agree that we are sinners and in need of a Savior. That is the first mountain lesson, a very important one.

The second one is Mount Zion, our spiritual, permanent home in heaven, the New Jerusalem. Here we see many people in joyful worship, close to God, in an intimate fellowship with Him and with each other. This is the mountain of grace in Christ, an extension of the cross of Calvary. The angels surround the throne and look with respect on the redeemed, each one the property of the Lamb. This mountain is our eternal and secure home, each of us having our name written on the gate of a mansion. Here the judge of all men is revealed as our father, changing and maturing righteous men into the perfect image of the First Born. We see light, joy, and singing. Here the best has triumphed over the good. The Kingdom of God among men, the Church, the Body, is established, secure and beautiful. Old things have passed away and everything has become new. Finally, Christ is all and in all.

These are the two kingdoms of God. The first one is temporary. The second one is eternal and ever increasing. We all start with the first. It is the shaking of God and the falling of the power of created things that will make a way for us to enter into the second. There is a personal shaking and deliverance. There is also a shaking that involves multitudes in the homes, churches, cities or nations, but the principle is always the same. There is a moment when you know in your spirit that you have to move on, to go to a higher place spiritually. It feels like you need to grow up, to mature and become fruitful. The Holy Spirit alone brings this desire for change. There is a season when He comes like a wind, dries and destroys the flesh and its desire to take the glory for success. This is a silent but powerful work that no man can do except the Spirit.

'The grass withers and the flower fall because the breath of the Lord blows on them' (Isaiah 40:7). This drying of flesh, this shaking, is the beginning of the genuine work of the Spirit in the heart of man. Many people that go to church lack this foundation. They are just religious, but not saved. They only know about Jesus from reading the Bible or books, without the saving faith that makes a man to be spirit. They have no idea that God shakes to rebuild or burns with fire to give 'beauty for ashes' at last.

Please pray that you may know the truth. Do not be satisfied with half prayers. Do not pray to impress men. Your very life, your ministry and destiny depends on what you ask God to give to you.

'Once more I will shake not only the earth but also the heavens. The words "once more" indicate the removing of what can be shaken – that is the created things – so that what cannot be shaken may remain' (Hebrews 12:26, 27).

As we continue to study prayer, we see that in Acts chapter 4, prayers were done until God answered. God answer through 'shaking' is the holy fire of judgment of God manifested in the circumstances. Everything changes miraculously. The created things were eliminated because they hindered the revelation of the unshakable Kingdom of God made of 'things that remain.' The word 'remain' in Greek means: to abide, to continue living in the residence without any interruptions. It is the power of the builder and the owner of the house, the power of the eternal dwelling within. The opposite is to be a visitor or a slave. Death has no influence upon things that abide. The things that 'remain' are not 'created' the way other material things exist on earth. They are established and sustained by the power of God within, who is the Creator of all things. This is a good place to stop and remind ourselves that the devil is a created being. 'You were blameless in your ways from the day you were created till wickedness was found in you' (Ezekiel 28:15). This is why all his works will be shaken and destroyed. The power of the devil, sin and death cannot survive God's judgment at the Cross. The grave could not hold Jesus. God judged all sin for all eternity when He came down, shook the ground and Jesus rose from the dead. On the third day there was 'a violent earthquake for an angel of the Lord came down from heaven…' the Roman soldiers became 'like dead men' (Matthew 28:2, 4). Forty days later Jesus ascended back to heaven. The disciples were given the promise that the Holy Spirit will come down in His name and establish their hearts as believers. About the devil Jesus said: "The prince of this world now stands condemned" (John 16:11).

THE UNSHAKABLE MAN

'Who may dwell in your sanctuary? Who may live on your holy hill? He whose walk is blameless and who does what is righteous… he will never be shaken.' 'Blessed is the man who fears the Lord, who finds great delight in his commands… Surely he will never be shaken…' (Psalms 15; 112).

In the Word of God we see described two types of men: the ones who shake off and the ones who remain standing. The first group is made of all men who are not saved; the other ones are men of the Spirit, the true believers, filled with the Holy Spirit. There is nothing interesting about the first group of people because we are all born sinners. We shall study the second group. These are the men who have died to sin, to the world, to the devil. Their identity is found in Christ alone and in His unshakable kingdom. We shall study Psalms 15 and 112 for this purpose. What are the main virtues of this man of God who never shakes?

HE AND HIS FAMILY LIVE IN GOD'S HOUSE FOR-EVER

'He who dwells in the secret place of the Most High shall remain stable and fixed under the shadow of the Almighty (Whose power no foe can withstand)' (Psalm 91:1, AMP).

This is the most important observation about the man of God. He has 'a permanent address'; he is established in the Spirit. He has his own spot and the promise of his own descendants. In other words he is settled and fruitful. All these are spiritual words and you need the Holy Spirit to understand them. To the natural mind, all what I am saying here is complete foolishness. But if you are saved, you may come to the place of maturity when you gain the blessed revelation of the assurance of salvation. The Holy Spirit will impart in you this strange peace that passes understanding that you and your house will serve the Lord forever. The promise God made to David will be your inheritance also: 'The Lord declares to you that the Lord himself will establish a house for you" (2 Samuel 7:11).

It is very useful to look at all the scriptures where you see the words 'establish, abide, remain, rest, endure…'; these all speak about eternal blessings that nothing can destroy, not even death. The man that never shakes has a permanent position in Christ where he abides forever; that is his home, his identity. This place is called 'the sanctuary, the holy hill' of God. He lives in God's house, but he is not a tenant. God calls him a son. He knows the truth. He is not a slave or a hireling living in the house temporarily. As a son, he belongs to the family of God forever (John 8:31-36). He is free from all sin or fears, especially doubt about his position in Christ. He understands his responsibilities and privileges in the family of God. This is a strong assurance that stabilizers his heart. That is why he is not 'moved.' He believes the promise of Jesus who says: 'I will make (him) a pillar in the temple of my God. Never again will he leave it!" (Revelation 3:12). By the mouth of Jesus 'never means never'!

This type of faith, to know your position in Christ, is not something you can manufacture or claim by human power or wisdom. No amount of human 'encouragement to believe' is enough. This faith is imparted by the Holy Spirit in 'the DNA' of the children of God alone. The assurance of a home forever cannot be found in this world. Here on earth things change and fade. If any man buys a new house today after sometime the house becomes old. Then there are taxes to pay until death. The foreigners and the tenants pay taxes, not the sons. That is why a man who owns a house in this world can never have quiet peace and strength of permanent abiding in one blessed spot. There is an anxiety that he may be rejected, that he may lose his house and family and that he may become nobody again… this is part of the natural system and all sinners know it too well. This is not so with the man of God who belongs to Christ. His position and his identity are God's gift to him forever. That is strength!

HIS HEART IS ESTABLISHED WITH DEED TO PROVE HIS FAITH IN GOD

Looking back at Psalms 15 and 112 we see the description of a mature believer. His heart is called established or fixed. These words in Hebrew mean to be faithful, patient, ordained by God to stand in His presence. It also means to be a leader, to be strong enough so that others may find in him support and rest. This man is described as good, humble, generous and courageous. He is a warrior on behalf of a good father to his children. He has received authority from Christ as a reward for his faithfulness. He actively serves God and impacts his generation. People remember him long after he is gone. He is a man of holy action with fruits to prove his choices in his personal life. His life is not just religious; it is not just words, especially when under provocation. Like Job of old, he has decided not to sin with his lips. He speaks the truth in love always. He does not hurt another so that he can be promoted, he does not slander, nor does he bribe to gain benefits. The honor he receives is from God and he humbly acknowledges that by giving Him all the glory. O... may we desire to be like this man of God and pay the price for this blessing! Families, cities and nations will be impacted by our testimony of faith. This is to be like Jesus Christ and there is no greater wish than this!

The conclusion is that the Word of God and all things of the Holy Spirit can never be shaken, ignored or forgotten. They are eternal because they are of God. All other things are created by God to be temporary. They will not stand the test of time or the test of fire of the judgment of God. This is the eternal Word of God that abides forever!

CHAPTER SEVEN

THE MOUNTAIN IN THE SEA

HAVE FAITH IN GOD

"And Jesus answering saith unto them have faith in God. For verily I say unto you that whosoever shall say unto this mountain 'Be thou removed and be thou cast into the sea' and shall not doubt in his heart, but shall believe that those things which he saith shall come to pass, he shall have whatsoever he saith. Therefore I say unto you, what things whatsoever ye desire, when ye pray, believe that ye receive them, and ye shall have them. And when you stand praying, forgive if ye have ought against any, that your Father also which is in heaven may forgive your trespasses. But if ye do not forgive, neither will your Father which is in heaven forgive your trespasses."

~Mark 11:22 - 26

This is a passage in the Bible that has greatly challenged me and encouraged me at the same time. I cannot say that I have exhausted its understanding. But I decided to write down the revelation that I have so far, trusting God that it will be of help to many. Amen! I want to see it as a practical advice to improve your prayer life and to increase your faith in God so that your silent dreams and desires in your heart may be fulfilled, all to the glory of God!

The scriptures above describe a conversation between Jesus and His disciples. The background is the miracle of the dried fig tree. The previous day Jesus 'was hungry' and He approached a fig tree hoping to find fruit. His 'desire' was to eat food. There was nothing except a lot of leaves. He then cursed the tree. The next day the disciples saw the tree dried from the roots and they remembered the curse. They were amazed at the power of such a word and hoped for an explanation. Then Jesus said that the secret of all authority is 'faith in God.'

Many books have been written about the subject of faith in God. It is not easy to explain, it is only the Holy Spirit that can really impart the knowledge of what faith is and what it is not. The definition of faith is trust; the ability to be loyal to God, to trust His character and His Word. Faith is the result of a spiritual relationship between the spirit of man and truth presented as it is found in the Word of God. Faith is the fruit that comes from trusting Christ for salvation; to trust and obey the Gospel of Christ. It means to profess Jesus Christ as Savior and Lord and it implies the constancy of this profession in all circumstances. False, religious faith trusts other things in the church but not Christ Himself. Selah!

DOUBT AND FEAR-THE ENEMIES OF FAITH

The opposite of faith is doubt and fear. Doubt is defined as the lack of confidence that hinders the will, the process of decision making. To doubt means to hesitate, to consider unlikely that there will be success ahead. Doubt has many questions with no answers that weaken the confidence to move forward trusting God for breakthrough. It is described in the Bible as staggering, wavering and stumbling or even a fall. It is a tendency to look back, to have a double mind or to backslide. A doubter has a strong tendency to reject truth and not to accept the Word of God. Fear is a 'sister' to doubt, a strong and unpleasant emotion because of a perceived or anticipated danger ahead. It manifests as loss of courage and confidence. It also weakens the will and the faith. The person who is reluctant to move ahead in life is very slow in making progress. He may look lazy or careless but the background may be fear of men, fear of the unknown, of visibility, or of failure.

Doubt can manifest as 'weak' faith. It is still doubt! Do not be deceived by it! It manifests as weakness of moving forward, a disability and a type of staggering and wavering of the spiritual 'ankles.' We are commanded to walk in faith; to 'strengthen our feeble arms and weak knees so that the lame may not be disabled, but rather healed' (Hebrews 12:12, 13). In other words, reject any form of weakness to your faith in God and His Word!

Doubt is crippling to 'the feet' and it affects the peace of mind. It creates anxiety. The feet are supposed to be protected by the shoes of the proclamation of the Gospel of peace who alone can destroy Satan (Ephesians 5:15; Romans 16:20). Doubt in the heart may be the reason why you cannot preach the true Gospel of Christ and you are always inclined to preach other things that cannot save the soul of man. Confront the evil spirit of doubt! Reject it!

A great example is Abraham, who did not get weak in his faith and 'did not waver through unbelief regarding the promise of God' (Romans 4:19, 20). Faith is always spoken as strength and healing. Be strong in Jesus' name, amen!

THE POWER OF THE SPOKEN WORD

'Whosoever shall say… and shall not doubt in his heart but believe that those things which he saith shall come to pass, he shall have whatsoever he saith' (Mark 11:23). What I see here is the power of the spoken word that comes with the authority of Christ. We are to be careful with the content of our hearts and the words that proceed from there. An empty heart speaks empty words; they may be beautiful or poetic, but empty nevertheless. A wicked and deceitful heart manifests itself by wicked words. Trying to correct or improve your speech without searching your heart is like doing cosmetic surgery on the face while the liver is filled with cancer. A beautiful corpse! Totally useless!

Jesus tells you to speak to a mountain that faces you, the big hindrance that blocks the path of progress. He says that the mountain can be removed and 'cast into the sea' so that there is freedom to move ahead. This great deliverance can be done by words of faith coming from a heart totally free from doubt. It is not enough to desire breakthrough. The conditions must be met according to the Word of God.

This scripture forces us to search our heart, the center of emotions and motives in serving God. Doubt is hiding and must be identified as 'a central' enemy. It has to be uprooted from there before you can see visible signs of breakthrough and healing. Remember, that 'the heart is deceitful above all things and beyond (human) cure' (Jeremiah 17:9). It will fight against the light so that it can retain the old 'tenant' of doubt. The battle is internal long before it becomes a visible victory. We are told to believe and eventually the desire will be manifested, it will 'come' to pass. This word in Hebrew means to become, to generate, to create, to perform and fulfill. This is a very important observation! True faith is the assurance to trust God as the Creator; that He can create something out of nothing; that He has no limitation to generate anything He pleases. True faith is trust in 'God who gives life to the dead and calls things that are not as though they were already there' (Romans 4:17). Doubt has fears that the invisible realm cannot become visible blessings. Faith has no fear like that. Faith trusts the God who is invisible, the God who is Spirit, to perform miracles, to bring into manifestation all things, spiritual or physical. 'Have faith in God'!

THE MOUNTAIN REMOVED AND CAST INTO THE SEA

What is this mountain? The definition is a conspicuous land mass above the surrounding plane. In Hebrew the word means something that lifts itself and blocks the way. It is a symbol of 'a proud thing that stands against the knowledge of God' (2 Corinthians 10:5). This mountain can be an accumulation of unresolved things from the past, a backlog of issues that have not been brought to the cross. Sin upon sin, it has grown to become a monster; especially the sin of un-forgiveness. That is why in the next verse Jesus brings the issue of sinful relationships, the hurt that follows them, piling up bitterness and guilt. The picture is of a mountain that disappears into the sea with a great crash and then becomes invisible. As long as the mountain of un-forgiveness is not repented of, if it is still visible, we will never make spiritual progress. On a positive note, forgiveness and reconciliation with God and others is the key that opens the door for miracles to happen. In a way, you have a choice between your 'pet' vengeance and the desire of your heart becoming a manifestation for God's glory.

THINGS YOU DESIRE… WHEN YOU PRAY… YOU SHALL HAVE THEM

How do you feel reading this promise? Someone asked me, how do you know that what you desire is the will of God? It is easy. When you pray and worship God… if the things you desire survive the fire of the Holy Spirit, then it is His will for you to have them. If the things you desire are consumed by the light of His presence, to the point that you even feel ashamed and guilty, then they are not of God.

The word 'desire' in Hebrew means to ask, to beg, to demand something due to you. It is more like the expectation of the promise of God, that what you desire should come to pass in your life according to His Word. It is also like the assurance that your faith in God is enough for the

36

manifestation to happen. Like Abraham, have the courage to trust God at His Word and against all odds, receive the promise (Romans 4:21). Learn to receive! Come to the place of faith and humility and just receive from God! DESIRE - PRAY-BELIEVE - HAVE THE MIRACLE!!! In Jesus' name, amen!

The subject of prayer is so great; sometimes I feel like swimming in the river of life that no man could cross (Ezekiel 47:2, 3). The scripture passage in Mark 11 chapters 22 to 26 is a treasure hidden in darkness. I have to trust God who graciously promised the revelation of such treasure and with the help of His Spirit, still 'dig' in for more. The light in the darkness will also level the mountains of sin along the way so that more treasures are exposed. This is God's promise! 'I will go before you and level the mountains... so that you may know that I am the Lord' (Isaiah 45:2, 3).

Getting back to the scripture in Mark 11, I just could not let go of it. The more I pondered, the more I saw that 'have faith in God' is not an easy command to obey. Like the saying goes, it is easier said than done. If it was an easy work, the disciples would not have been so surprised at the faith of Jesus. They were in His presence daily and still could not 'manufacture' the faith necessary to make a fig tree dry for lack of fruits. Earlier in the ministry, they tried to deliver a child from demon possession but failed to do so. Jesus said that they needed to spiritually prepare to fast and pray before they have enough faith to command a demon to depart with just a word. I agree with the father who said: Lord, "I do believe; help my unbelief" (Mark 9:24).

From these examples we see that there are two types of faith. The first one we shall call 'baby faith,' or 'seed faith.' This is a given gift when we trust God for salvation. Without this gift of grace from God we cannot be saved; we are just religious. This faith is 'a mustard seed' not yet planted in the ground of ministry. It has great potential but it has not multiplied in strength. It is just enough to save your soul but not enough to ignite miracles.

The second type of faith is called 'harvest faith.' The initial seed of faith was invested in the work of ministry and through trials and even mistakes, it becomes pure and strong. This is the harvest of righteousness that changes your circumstances and even the destiny of nations; the living faith, able to produce works, to the glory of God. This faith is the product of a mature, spiritual mind. It has the same quality with the faith of Jesus. Once you have this mature faith, prayer becomes a joy and Christianity an adventure led by the Spirit. Selah!

MATURE FAITH IS HAVING THE MIND OF CHRIST

'But we have the mind of Christ' (1 Corinthians 2:16).

'For verily I say unto you that whosoever shall say into this mountain 'Be thou removed and be thou cast into the sea' and shall not doubt in his heart...' In the latter scripture Jesus said that 'whosoever' can command a mountain of obstruction 'to be removed and cast into the sea,' having only faith and no doubt in his heart, that person will receive the manifestation of his heart's desire from God. Do not be surprised at this wonderful promise. God is a generous Person and there are other scriptures to prove that he cares for you and actively plans your personal happiness (Psalm 37:4, Ecclesiastes 5:18-20; 9:7-9). To open your mouth and command a mountain of obstruction to leave your path is easy to do. Why don't the mountains move? It is because our words are empty or contain doubt in them. God looks at the heart and listens to our words. We are not the judge of our own words. In fact we shall be judged for speaking any 'careless word' (Matthew 12:36, 37). The Greek meaning of 'careless' is to be idle, to be slow, and to be unemployed. One form of judgment for careless religious prayer is the lack of answers to the same prayers. Just writing these words, my heart is beating faster, as I try to understand the responsibility given to us as believers. What I see here is that only God can 'remove' a mountain from its position and to 'cast it into the sea.' God created the earth. It belongs to Him (Genesis 1:1; Psalm 24:1, 2). He placed mountains and hills at His pleasure where He wanted them to be. None can change the topography of this planet except its Creator. This is true.

I have heard of islands that experienced an earthquake and disappeared completely into the sea. Scientists may have their own explanations but I know that it is the power of God manifested in His creation to help us understand the privilege of faith. The mountain Jesus is talking about is spiritual. The change in the spiritual environment or atmosphere is done by God. The mighty change is also done by God's children who have the mind of Christ and who understand and apply His authority on earth! Selah! Ignorance of His authority is the door that permits doubt to

enter in the heart which wounds and weakens faith. That is why mountains do not move and we pray in vain for the manifestation of our desires.
In other words you have to be a child of God, filled with the Spirit, walking and led by the Spirit, dead to the flesh and sin, and alive in Christ and
His authority as the Ruler of the earth. If you fulfill these conditions,
hindrances are removed and disappear into the sea of forgetfulness. The
road ahead of you will become plain just like before Zerubbabel. Then
you shall have the privilege to crown your efforts with the capstone of
grace and give glory to God with shouts of 'God bless it'! That shout is
the visible manifestation of your heart's desires is an approval of your
calling into ministry. This is the commendation of God upon His faithful
servants. Miracles will be your portion!

'These signs will accompany those who believe: in my name they will
drive out demons, they will speak with new tongues... they will place
their hands on sick people and they will get well' (Mark 16:17, 18).
'What are you, O mighty mountain? Before Zerubbabel you will become
level ground... then you will know that the Lord Almighty has sent me
to you!' (Zechariah 3:7-9).

'In the morning, as they went along, they saw the fig tree withered
from the roots. Peter remembered and said to Jesus 'Rabbi, look! The fig
tree you cursed has withered! "have faith in God"- Jesus answered'
(Mark 11:20-22).

We have not exhausted the meaning of the scriptures in Mark chapter
11; let us look once more at the reason why Jesus commands us to have
faith that moves 'mountains' of difficulties. In particular let us examine
the connection between the withered fig tree and the command of faith,
because these are in the same chapter. It is Peter's amazement about the
withered tree that was the background of Jesus teaching about faith and
doubt. We have looked at these verses of faith more or less on their own.
But we cannot ignore the link with the events on that particular day. The
command to have faith in God was given under the shadow, or the lack
thereof, of the cursed, dry fig tree. So, what is the revelation here?

HOPELESS BARRENESS (Mark 11 and Luke 13)

Please read Mark 11; the whole chapter. At the beginning we see Jesus
entering Jerusalem as a King according to the prophecy (Zechariah 9:9).

Later in the day He goes to the temple and 'He looked around at everything.' In the evening Jesus and the disciples go to Bethany, possibly to the house of Martha and Mary, to rest for the night. It is there that He plans what to do in the temple. Early the next morning they come back towards Jerusalem and 'Jesus was hungry.' Suddenly He sees along the road, in the distance, a fig tree full of shiny leaves. He goes closer to look for fruit and He finds none. Mark said that it was not 'the season for figs.' Nevertheless Jesus curses the tree by speaking to it: 'May no one ever eat fruit from you again.' That sounded strange to the disciples. Then they move on to the city. In the temple, Jesus does something even more strange. He overturns and scatters the tables of all who were buying and selling there saying: 'My house will be called a house of prayer for all nations. But you have made it a den of robbers.' These are quotations from the prophets Isaiah and Jeremiah combined. He stops all traffic and business in the temple for a few hours. Later in the day, they go back on the same road and Peter is surprised to see the fig tree 'withered from the roots.' He expresses his amazement that just a word from Jesus was enough to destroy a strong tree so quickly. In other words, Peter manifests his silent doubt. That is why Jesus commands him to have faith in God. This is the place where the disciples are told about the mountain of hindrance and the faith that can remove it. Then Jesus identifies lack of love and forgiveness as the greatest barrier on the road of faith. This is the story in general. Let's look now at some details.

The first thing that is difficult to explain is why Jesus got so angry with the barren tree, especially when it was not harvest time. For many years I did not understand this passage. I recently found a wonderful explanation in an old book called *The Barren Fig Tree* by W.M. Christie, a missionary in Palestine. He said that the fig trees that grow in Israel have a special pattern of producing fruits. In the spring time, the second half of the month of March the trees bring out leaves. With the appearance of the foliage there is also the emergence of some little green fruit. These are not the figs, but something that resembles them; the forerunners are called 'taqsh.' They are the size of almonds and they are edible. They are not very sweet, but the shepherds eat them when they are very hungry. What is interesting is that the number of these pre-fruits predicts the harvest later, at the end of April. Jesus was crucified in the second week of April. The cursing of this tree was possibly done a week earlier. That is why Mark said that it was not yet the time for figs. But Jesus expected to see at least some 'taqsh' on the tree. This is the revelation: The green big leaves that 'advertised' the tree were a cover up for a total and hopeless barrenness; the picture of an old religious hypocrite, just like the ones Jesus found in the temple and overturned their tables. In this chapter we see Jesus as Man and as God. In His hunger, we see Jesus as the Son of Man. In cursing the barren tree, we see Him as the owner and the judge of creation. He alone knows if there is absolutely no future for a tree or man and He has the right to uproot any that is only a waste to His resources on earth.

In Luke 13 there is another parable, the picture of a fig tree planted in the middle of a vineyard. For three years the owner comes expecting fruit but he finds none. He then orders to cut down the barren fig tree because it is more than useless, it is a continuous waste. 'Why should it use up the soil?' the caretaker asks for one more year of intensive labor. If at the end of the forth year there is no fruit, then the tree is proven to be hopelessly barren; it will be cut down and replaced with another. In this parable God is the owner and Jesus is the caretaker. The vineyard stands for the congregation of the believers in the church. The fig tree in the middle represents the religious man that goes to church. He hears the gospel preached, if he refuses to repent he will surely 'perish' (Luke 13:3-5). Just like the man who came to the wedding feast but refused the owner's gift of free clothes, he is in danger of being sent into darkness of perdition (Matthew 22:11-13). Repentance must be proved with visible fruits of a changed character. It is not enough to just attend 'a good church.' This is a warning from heaven: Religious people have a limited time of favor to become humble and repent. God does not give them an indefinite number of options; life itself on earth is short. Taking the grace of God for granted and resisting the Spirit will eventually bring down God's judgment with 'fire' (Matthew 3:8-10). God shows Jeremiah two types of figs: good and very bad. There are only two types of people according to God: believers and unbelievers. The good ones are God's children and He blesses them. The bad figs will be destroyed for refusing to listen and obey God's word (Jeremiah 24, 29:17-19). No man can 'disappoint' God and live. For example, when a man plants an orange tree he expects oranges in the near future. Everything God does is with a purpose. If the tree does not produce figs according to His expectations, He has the right to destroy that tree. This is the right of the owner! God is the owner of everything! When Jesus cursed the tree in Mark 11, He proved to be God, the owner of that tree and everything on earth. The disciples were not surprised when Jesus was hungry as a man. But they were surprised when He exercised authority as God. The evil religious spirit of doubt is revealed by not acknowledging Jesus Christ as the Creator, Owner, and the Judge of all the earth. It is the revelation of the spirit of antichrist according to 1 John 4:2, 3. The spirit of religion will never satisfy your hunger for God. Please pray that your eyes are open to see the truth so that you may be free.

Leaves on a tree symbolize the works of the flesh. Adam and Eve used the leaves from the fig tree to sew their clothes. But they could not hide the nakedness and shame of sin. The blood of the Lamb had to be shed for God to use its skin to make a real covering for them (Genesis 2:7; 3:21).

As leaves stand for the works of the flesh, fruits stand for the work of the Holy Spirit in the human heart. This is a very important principle. Selah! The lesson here is to examine our lives and see if we are fruitful and if the Holy Spirit has been allowed free access to do His work in our hearts. The visible and edible spiritual fruit in our lives is the proof of the power of resurrection working within. This 'working out your salvation' (Philippians 2:12, 13) is a great achievement for any believer to intimately know that power. It is the true seal of God's love, the kiss of Jesus upon your spirit. The edible fruit of the Holy Spirit available to feed others is spiritual ministry indeed! "My lover spoke and said to me: Arise my darling, my beautiful one and come with me. See! The winter is past... The fig tree forms its early fruit the blossoming vines spread their fragrance. Arise, come..." (Song of Songs 2:10-13). The only fruit that God recognizes and gives Him glory is called fruit 'that remains' (John 15:16). The word remains means to abide uninterrupted, to continue without fading or spoiling. Good figs can never become bad. This spiritual harvest survives our short life on earth. It contributes to the increase and to the glory of the Kingdom of God. The value of these eternal fruits is beyond human understanding. If we appreciate the pleasure of God, we should desire passionately to be spiritually fruitful. God is very particular about fruits. Read John 15 and see. He cuts off any branch that is barren. He prunes the ones that are fruitful so that the production will increase. Spiritual fruit in your life is a proof of your unity with Christ and your assurance of salvation.

Let's go back to Mark 11. The mountain to be removed by faith from this point of view is the power of flesh that kills the desire for spiritual fruitfulness. It is the stronghold of doubt deceiving you that it is your 'destiny' to be unmarried or barren forever. This mountain blocks your vision to become spiritually mature. 'Have faith in God,' for He has given the Son His authority to judge the earth (John 5:22, 23).

Salt that loses its saltiness is useless. In the same way, a religious hopelessly barren, rebellious and stubborn man that comes to church, but frustrates the grace of God is a waste and in danger of being replaced by another. In particular, the un-willingness to love and forgive others is the greatest poison to life and spiritual growth.

Oh, that your eyes be opened to see the truth that sets us free indeed! Amen!

CHAPTER EIGHT

SIN OF DOUBT

AN ENEMY OF FAITH

"If any of you lacks wisdom, he should ask God who gives generously to all without finding fault, and it will be given him. But when he asks, he must not doubt because he who doubts is like the wave of the sea, blown and tossed by the wind. That man should not think he will receive any-thing from the Lord; he is a double minded man, unstable in all he does."
~James 1: 5 - 8

Before we look at the latter scripture, let us read some descriptions of doubt that will reveal the doubters heart:

- To be undecided; to find yourself always at crossroads on the path of life and never on a straight and simple road;
- To hesitate in making a choice for fear of failure; to waste time, to waver because success is seen as unlikely;
- To have a weak will, a tendency to look back after making a decision, the fear of backsliding is always a shadow;
- To have weak faith, unwilling to believe without clear or visible proof; hard to trust the promises of God;
- To expect failure at first, then possible, little success at last;
- To lack the courage to be happy in your personal life;
- To have a tendency to postpone actions until some imaginary conditions are met;
- To yield to another's wishes, a voluntary submitting of the will to another out of respect, intimidation or 'love';
- To surrender the control of your will, to foolishly relinquish your position of advantage to another;
- To give up all resistance against evil and to acknowledge the superiority of another;

45

- To agree that you are inferior, that you are a loser, and a failure; in total opposition with the Word of God.

Getting back to James 1, we see that the man who doubts is described as 'a wave of the sea, blown and tossed by the wind.' The sea is very deep. Its waves change only the surface, its color, and movement, depending on the intensity of the wind. Just like the sea, the doubter has deep fears and weaknesses, hidden from the eyes of men. The only thing we see, just like the moving waves, is that he is unstable in all his choices and actions. You can't trust a doubter. He can't even trust himself. This instability is the result of weak faith, a lack of rest and trust in the promises of God.

James describes the doubter in connection with the prayer for divine wisdom. The biblical definition of wisdom is the skill to apply the Word of God in practical life and in the daily choices that we make. Wisdom is not intelligence and it is not education. It is a gift from God. It is not how many scriptures you have memorized. It is the 'few' scriptures you know that have given you testimonies from their application. That is wisdom from above. We are assured that God is willing and generous to impart wisdom when we need it. It means that the doubter is not just double minded, but he is a double fool. His doubt is a hindrance against wisdom, against the application of the Word in his life. He lacks personal testimony as a believer. He is just religious. The mountain of accumulated wrong choices has to be cast into the sea. In other words, the believer has to challenge and doubt his own doubts. Ask yourself some questions in the presence of God!

Why am I so afraid to trust God? What do I lose if I believe? Why do I waste so much time when I know that I should move ahead in life? Why do I fear what others will say if I fail in trusting God? Why can't I be happy with God's promises? What do I really want from God that He did not give me? What if I qualify as a doubter in the Bible? Why do I feel like resisting the truth and the act of repentance to change? Why is it that all these years I have foolishly resisted truth instead of resisting the lies of the devil? What if a seed of doubt has been planted long ago by a wicked evil spirit? Why do I always feel like a failure? Why do I fear men? Why am I so weak spiritually? Why are some of my prayers not answered? What if God is showing mercy to me by revealing these things for me?

I take authority in the name of Jesus against any evil spirit of doubt and unbelief that has influenced my mind all these years!!! I resist your lies and I reject you in the name of Jesus! I plead the Blood of Jesus and I claim the victory that Christ won for me at the cross! Holy Spirit come and fill me completely! In Jesus' name I pray, amen!

THE RIGHTEOUSNESS OF FAITH- NO DOUBTING

'But Abram said: 'O Sovereign Lord what can you give me since I remain childless and the one who will inherit my estate is Eliezer of Damascus?' Then the word of the Lord came to him: 'This man will not be your heir, but a son coming from your own body will be your heir. Look at the heavens and count the stars- if indeed you can count them- so shall your offspring be.' Abram believed the Lord and he credited to him as right-eousness' (Genesis 15:2-6).

Here we see a glimpse of the prayer life of Abraham, God's friend. As we have seen, prayer is a two way discussion and fellowship with God. It is never a monologue. If God does not answer your prayers, if He does not correct and encourage you through the means of your prayers, it means that you are just talking religion to yourself. That is not prayer. Please take note: God 'edits' the prayers of His children. He does not delete prayers done in Jesus' name. One of the Titles of Jesus is 'The Patient Collector of our prayers' (Revelations 8). Having this revelation should encourage you to pray more, not less.

Before Genesis 15, Abraham did not talk directly to God. He obeyed silently, with actions but did not open his heart and mouth to God. This is the first time that he talks to God, expressing his fears about the future, the first time he prays to God!

Since Abraham obeyed God's command to leave his father's house, God had been faithful to the promise He made to him. Abraham became rich and famous, beyond his imagination. His friends and servants were blessed and his enemies defeated. Some years had passed and he had time to think about his relationship with God. He clearly observed that God is a Person who was kind to him, faithful and powerful. So he makes up his mind that the next time God comes close to him with another wonderful promise of blessings; he would remember to open his heart and his mouth! He would pray! He would express his secret fear of dying childless and that all his property, all the blessings from God would be inherited by a stranger. His servant Eliezer was a faithful man and he had served him well all these years. But still, he was a stranger, a Syrian from Damascus. Could God be so careless with the future of his blessings given to His 'friend'? Is it possible that all labor and great inheritance will be given to another? - What does it mean to be the founder of a 'great nation'? Could that nation be a gathering of his servants and household slaves? No children? No sons? No daughter...' –Abraham thought silently. This was a picture of Abraham's heart prepared for the baptism of prayer. Years passed... still waiting... Then suddenly God speaks: 'Do not be afraid, Abram. I am your shield; your very great reward' (Genesis 15:1). That was the moment! - Abraham thought to himself. God is speaking again, this time assuring him of total protection from enemies, a future reward, a payment, a compensation for past faithfulness... more blessings... more promises...

To Abraham, this new promise, as wonderful as it seemed, appeared to useless in the absence of children. What kind of a reward will gladden the heart of an old man without children to inherit it after his death? He decided to open his mouth and speak to God... better said, to pray with faith! He addressed God as Sovereign Lord, Jehovah the God who does what He pleases and none can oppose. As he worshipped God he struggled to open his heart, to find words to explain his pain... an old man, rich and blessed, afraid that he may be ungrateful, but still... no children to carry on his legacy... Abraham prays... 'What can you give me...?' immediately God answers his prayer! He promises that he will surely have a son coming from his own loins and his descendants will be uncountable; they will inherit the earth. Abraham makes a choice that will determine his destiny and that of his descendants. What was that decision? Abraham believed God who freely and graciously promised these blessings and had the power to perform them. Abraham decided that henceforth he will trust God's word and not doubt at all until he sees with his own eyes the manifestation of the promise. It is on record that he 'Without weakening in his faith he faced the fact that his body was as good as dead... and that Sarah's womb was also dead. Yet, he did not waver through unbelief regarding the promise of God but strengthened in his faith and gave glory to God, being fully persuaded that God has the power to do what he has promised' (Romans 4:19-21). This is called the royal seal of righteousness by faith (Romans 4:11) – the approval of the Holy Spirit upon a man who lives and dies trusting God to the end.

You can see that there is a point in time when you know beyond any shadow of doubt that God is speaking to you about your future. At that very point God expects a quality decision to trust His promise 'against all hope.' That trust implies that you recognize the weakness of your flesh and you ask the same God to strengthen you in your choice of faith and against doubt. You have to invest your initial faith, like a seed in prayer, back to God, for Him to protect you against what is called the spiritual 'wavering' of doubt. That is wisdom. This is what 'Abraham discovered in this matter' (Romans 4:1) and we have to do the same.

TO WAVER SPIRITUALLY – DEFINITION

- It means to stagger up and down, to go zigzag, to go round in circles, to deviate from the original purpose of the action.
- It means to be a coward, to draw back emotionally because of fear or hate to confront the obstacle ahead.
- It means to hesitate, to pause from moving ahead with the intent of judging God's plans and His love for you (suddenly you fear that God is pushing you into danger and disgrace and abandoning you there).
- It means to go between two opinions and allegiances (you said you love God but now, even the devil does not sound so bad…).
- It means to be surprised and unprepared when unexpectedly you receive a blow from outside; for a moment you lose your balance, the control of mind and emotions, enough for the seed of doubt to be planted in your heart.

This attack without warning leaves you weaker, confused, shocked, dizzy, angry, and in fear. You foolishly blame God for it. You start drowning in self-pity, frustrated and defeated in your desire to obey God. You say to yourself; "This is not what I have hoped for!" The reflex of survival comes in and you start thinking of going back from the position of faith. You start to stagger, looking back for the help that is found only when moving ahead…

This is how the enemy attacks faith in the promises of God. Abraham protected his spirit prudently by anticipating this type of warfare. It is called the trial of faith. With a royal stamp, God seals them that pass this warfare successfully, and uses them as examples for others to follow.

49

It is safe to say that any word, any promise, any hope that is not followed by direct confrontation from the evil spirit of doubt is not from God. We are commanded to rejoice when tempted by doubt so that we learn to resist it and become spiritually mature. God rewards his faithful children who like Abraham persevere in faith until the spiritual, invisible promise becomes a visible manifestation, to the glory of God who purposed it. Abraham's faith became stronger and stronger. Each defeated attack helped him to gain the confidence that indeed God is worthy to be trusted to the end and that there will be a performance of the things spoken by God. He learned over time to identify with God and saw doubt as an enemy. With the help of the Spirit he resists and rejects doubt in daily choices and turns the pains of temptation into praise, giving glory to God! God called him the father of many nations. We claim by faith that Abraham is the father of all nations. What a testimony! What a challenge! What a heritage we have!

'These (trials) have come so that your faith – of greater worth than gold, which perishes even though refined by fire – may be proved genuine and may result in praise, glory and honor when Jesus Christ is revealed... even though you do not see him now, you believe in him and are filled with inexpressible and glorious joy... receiving the goal of your faith...' (1Peter1:7-9).

'Blessed is the man who perseveres under trial (of faith), because when he has stood the test, he will receive the crown of life that God has promised to those who love him' (James 1:12).

'Blessed is she who has believed that what the Lord has said will be accomplished... for there shall be a performance' (Luke 1:45). Amen!

As we continue the study of doubt as a hindrance to prayer; let us look in the Book of Luke, chapter 1. Here we are told that the Angel Gabriel was sent to deliver the good news of a miraculous conception to two people, one old and the other young. We shall study and compare their reactions so that we may learn to respond in faith and to reject doubt, all to the glory of God.

DOUBT MEANS DELAYED, PARTIAL AND GRUDGING RESPONSE TO GOD'S WORD

Zechariah was an old man, but had no child. Surely he and Elizabeth prayed for many years that God would remove the shame of barrenness from them. So many years had passed that he assumed they were too old to receive an answer to their prayer. Surely, he knew about Abraham, the father of his faith; how long he waited for a son. But somehow, he got tired of trusting in the promises of God. He thought that no one understood his pain and he thought that he would die a disappointed man. He continued to be a priest, but ministry became just religious routine and life had no joy. All around him was only defeat, fear, darkness, and the shadow of death. He was a Levite priest taking care of God's Temple.

In this particular day, he was chosen to offer the incense on the altar. Because the Levites are many, the chance of being selected to enter the Holy Place was very small. This was a great privilege, to leave the crowd of worshippers outside the gate and to go alone and meet with God. We do not know all that was in Zechariah's mind as he entered the Holy Place with the incense and fire in his hands. What we know is that he was spiritually unprepared for the encounter with God's messenger. In the dim, mysterious light coming from the golden lamp stand, he was shocked to see someone standing on the right side of the altar of incense. It is possible that the angel looked like an ordinary man, but his presence could not be ordinary. Zechariah knew that none could enter the Holy Place and survive the glory inside except the one approved by God.

The first thing the angel says to him is 'Fear not!' That is the best news any sinner can ever hear. It is the gospel of Christ! The angel tells him that his prayers of long ago have been answered; that they will have a son who will be a great blessing to many. The boy's name will be John. He will be a prophet who will prepare the people of God for the coming of the Messiah. At the end of this prophetic and encouraging speech, suddenly Zechariah expresses his silent doubts 'How can I be sure of this...'? Immediately, the angel restrains the doubt of the priest passing judgment. For almost a year Zechariah will be dumb, 'unable to speak' until the fulfillment of this prophecy. In silence, he will have enough time to meditate and repent of his sin of unbelief, of doubt and of fear. The word 'dumb' in Greek means to be silent, to be mute – but not deaf; to have a weak tongue, the loss of power to perform, to talk or to be active.

God expects us to obey, to react with immediate faith and joy when we hear His Word. A slow, hesitant answer is counted as doubt and immediately something happens to the soul. A veil of darkness will soon cover it. The thinking becomes slow and difficult, dull and foolish. The mind is unable to appreciate, understand or retain knowledge, especially spiritual things (2Corinthians 3:14-4; 4). This is the judgment of God upon the sin of doubt. Slowly, the believer backslides and drifts away from the truth, losing spiritual discernment as doubt settles in. This is a spiritual principle: if truth and faith are rejected, then deception, fear and doubt will surely enter the heart (Deuteronomy 28:47, 48; Romans 2:1-26; 2 Thessalonians 2:10-12; Hebrews 5:11). Selah!

Let's look at Mary's answer to the angel and contrast her attitude with Zechariah's. His first words to her are the same: 'Fear not'! Then the angel speaks God's word to her: she will have a baby boy named Jesus, a King and a Savior. She too responds with the same question: 'How will this be…since I am a virgin?' the words are similar with Zechariah's, but the hearts are different. The lesson here is that you cannot, in the natural, discern the true believer from the mere religious one. God, who alone knows the hearts, qualifies Mary's response to be faith and the other doubt. Mary was a young girl, not married and having a child was not her priority. But immediately she heard the word, she trusted God that there will be 'a performance' of His spoken word. Doubt fails to believe that the invisible Word of God in the form of preaching, prophecy or prayer, will become a visible manifestation of a miracle! Doubt does not see the connection between the Spirit realm and the natural.

Zechariah was 'an upright' man, a true believer. He was a religious man, a priest all his life, possibly in full time ministry. He was also a man who had a need that only God could supply. He had to meditate upon the word of God and many opportunities to meet with God in the temple. With all these blessings, he was still harboring a secret doubt in his heart, even when he was in the presence of God. The only explanation is that Zechariah was deceived in the past and opened his heart to the evil spirit of religion who mixed doubt with his faith. God is merciful and does not cancel the blessing of an answered prayer; the promised baby will be born. Possibly Elizabeth did not stop believing God for the child. But, God through the angel did not just overlook the sin of doubt. Judgment of silence is given for the next one year. Repentance is necessary; the speech is restored by God to give Him honor and praise! In 'due season' John is born and the mercy of God is revealed. The tongue of Zechariah is loosed once more. He is still an old man, but so different… Filled with the Holy Spirit and he is ready to praise Jehovah, his God, his Savior and Redeemer!

'Blessed is she that believed for there shall be a performance of those things which were told her from the Lord' (Luke 1:45; KJV). This is true faith! Selah!

DOUBT GRIEVES THE HOLY SPIRIT

'Ask (pray to) the Lord your God for a sign… Hear now you house of David! Is it not enough to try the patience of men? Will you try the patience of my God also? The Lord Himself will give you a sign. The virgin will be with child and will give birth to a son and will call him Immanuel' (Isaiah 7:11-14).

The story of Zechariah and Mary described above, has its roots in a prophecy given by Isaiah hundreds of years previously. We find it in the Book of Isaiah, chapter seven. Here we see a great revelation about true faith contrasted with the sin of doubt. King Ahaz of Judah is under attack. He and all the people panic at the sure defeat. He goes to inspect the Upper Pool, possibly to see if the reserve of water will be enough in case of war. That speaks of self-confidence. He is a proud and wicked king who deserves no mercy. But we see that God encourages him to trust in Him alone and the victory will be sure. We see here that our God is a God of covenant, merciful and faithful even with sinners.

Faith helps you to stand; doubt weakens you until you fall. 'If you do not stand firm in your faith, you will not stand at all' (Isaiah 7:9). Faith is God's command and the only option for righteousness, for pleasing Him. God commands Ahaz to pray, to ask for a sign that will strengthen his faith. In other words God tells him that he must ask to be filled with the Holy Spirit, the Encourager. But Ahaz thinks that more encouragement is unnecessary, trusting that his faith is strong enough. That is when God gets angry and rebukes him for 'trying His patience.' The phrase in Hebrew means to weaken or to grieve someone. The lesson is this: religious faith is weak faith and it is polluted; it is mixed with doubt and fear, and it grieves God, the Holy Spirit.

God sovereignty overrules Ahaz's foolishness and gives a sign that will forever strengthen the faith of all believers, to the end of time. It is called Immanuel, 'God is with us.' It is a miraculous sign that God knows what we need. God recommends the revelation of Immanuel as a sign to establish our faith. Spiritually speaking, Ahaz is commanded to remove his attention and trust from the Water Pool and 'to look unto Jesus, the author and finisher of our faith' (Hebrews 12:2). We are commanded to look away from self-confidence, which is pride, the result of doubting God, and to behold the beauty and power of Jesus our Savior and Lord. Then all fear is gone! Then faith is established and doubt is forever defeated in our hearts!

When the enemy came to attack Jerusalem he was shocked to discover that 'God is within her – she will never fall' (Psalm 46:5).

The old priest Zechariah, the father of John, should have remembered the eternal sign of Immanuel. His son was to prepare the way before the Messiah as a fulfillment of the prophecy on Isaiah 7.

Do you believe that the presence of God with you is the only protection you need? This is the Word of God! If you doubt it and you look for the help of man, you will surely fall during times of trials.

O... the presence of God the Holy Spirit in the heart of the believer... Immanuel sign and seal...eternal encouragement!

DOUBT IS THE RELIGION OF THE COWARD AND THE FAITH OF THE FOOL

'See to it brothers that none of you has a sinful, unbelieving heart that turns away from the Living God' (Hebrews 3:12).

Doubt is not very easy to detect. It is hidden behind much church work, many prayers, and religious activities. If you do not confront it to come out of hiding, you can never discover it accidentally. When there is doubt in the heart, it takes a long time to find out that your gain is minimal; that there is very little harvest in comparison with the effort invested. Faith in the Word of God is described as a double edged sword or a sharp iron axe combined with the skill to use them as tools or weapons. Doubt is the opposite. It is a blunt axe that fails in time of need and it requires too much strength to be useful. Doubt will make you slow and lazy, a serious danger in warfare. Prayer of doubt will make you to be tired spiritually and physically. That is why doubters like entertainment, but hate prayer meetings (Ecclesiastes 10:10, 11; Hebrews 4:12).

Doubt makes the mind sluggish and lazy. It is spiritual laziness that makes the believer superficial with the study of the Word and prayer. It is foolishness; a lack of understanding of spiritual things. The revelation of the Spirit is by definition 'deep,' like gold hidden in the ground. It requires spiritual labor to find it (1 Corinthians 2:10). Doubt is the greatest hindrance to spiritual maturity.

Below are some of the warning signs (spiritual and physical) of hidden doubt in the heart of the believer:

- The believer finds that he has no joy, no peace, no rest, no confidence, no focus, no identity, no spiritual growth – Christianity is not 'sweet';
- All around the believer only sees poverty, lack of good things, always in need; work seems like slavery – his account is never 'balanced';
- He is very slow, has difficulty progressing; things getting worse and eventually a full stop of progress in life – boring life;
- The believer also has much disappointment, bitterness, sad wasted hopes and dream – and the feeling of being 'too old' to succeed;
- He often misses opportunities for ministry and for doing good – feeling 'cheated' in life;
- He is perpetually going in circles, making many foolish mistakes, with a complicated and confused life – He feels that God has forgotten him; and he has no breakthroughs;
- He often gives up the fight; feeling like a failure - He forgets the taste of sweet royal victory;
- He constantly feels jealous, hating those who have faith and grow spiritually – He does not experience miracles in my life... (Proverbs 12:24; 15:19; 19:24; 21:25; 22:13; 24:30-34; 26:14).

May our prayers and blessings never be hindered by doubt and fear. May we always choose to believe God's promises are yes and amen! In Jesus' name, amen!

Pray Ye

CHAPTER NINE

HINDRANCES TO PRAYER

CHERISHED SIN

"Surely the arm of the Lord is not too short to save, nor his ear too dull to hear. But your iniquities have separated you from God; your sins have hidden his face from you."

~Isaiah 59: 1, 2

The devil hates it when a believer comes close to God for prayer or worship. It is not easy to persevere in prayer until the answer comes. Much of the opposition is designed to discourage us, to look for other ways to solve our problems. The devil does not care if you work harder at making your life a 'success.' He is happy if you are deceived in replacing prayer with other things. Many believers have stumbled in this way and have lost their passion to meet with the Lord in prayer. Remember this: we should pray more often, with more faith and passion, not less!

This is a simple doctrine: Sin separates from God! Sin connects with the world and destroys the intimacy with God. Sin is breaking God's law; it is rebellion against God. In Hebrew and Greek sin is defined as a habitual offence, an imperfection, a trespass and a leading astray; a crime with its guilt and its punishment. Sin is described as 'missing the mark'; the greatest eternal disappointment. It is like going into a competition with great hopes to win the precious prize and die in the attempt. You lose your greatest dreams and others will carry them away.

What is God's purpose for His creation in general and man in particular? It is to give glory to God and to be conformed to the image of God's Son, Jesus Christ. The Westminster Catechism asks this question: 'What is the chief end of man?' The answer given is: 'To glorify God and enjoy Him forever.' Therefore sin is an eternal and total failure to fulfill God's plan and purpose for man who will never know, worship, and pray to God. The entrance of sin is the greatest tragedy known to mankind. A sinful man tries to know, worship, and pray to God. This attempt is called religion. Religion is sin. No man can know God through any religion. God has revealed Himself to man only through Jesus Christ. Salvation is only through Jesus Christ. Fellowship and prayer is accepted only because of the cross. The Blood of the Lamb has been shed for us to be able to pray. Having paid the price, Jesus is now the High Priest in Heaven, Faithful Collector of our prayers and intercessions. See how great the privilege of prayer is! Sin separated us from God. Jesus became sin so that we could become the righteousness of God, and so that we can pray. It is a mystery that no human mind can explain: Jesus, who knew not sin, became sin for us (2 Corinthians 5:21)! It is at the cross that the curse of sin was destroyed. We were 'separated from Christ, excluded from citizenship in Israel and foreigners of the covenants of the promise, without hope and without God in the world' (Ephesians 2:12).

At the Cross, the Door of Christ was opened and we came in. Once sin is confessed and repented of, and the unity of the Spirit is restored then prayer becomes as 'natural' as breathing, an expression of God's love for His child. The Cross is the greatest victory on behalf of mankind!

"At the Cross, at the Cross where I first saw the light and the burden of my heart rolled away…" O, the blessed moment when I trusted Jesus as my Savior and Lord! The fence of division, shame and rejection became the bridge of hope. I remember the moment when I said… no, I cried from within: 'Abba Father'! The Spirit of adoption became the Spirit of prayer and supplication. My breath became the fragrance of Christ and my heart beat a flood of prayer. My mouth could not resist the sweet aroma of utterance so precious to God. My first prayer! The hour that I first believed! So simple, and yet, so wonderful! "If I had cherished sin in my heart, the Lord would not have listened; but God has surely listened and heard my voice in prayer. Praise be to God, who has not rejected my prayer or withheld his love from me!" (Psalm 66:18-20)

IDOLS IN THE HEART

"Then the Word of the Lord came to me 'Son of man, these men have set up idols in their hearts and put wicked stumbling blocks before their faces. Should I let them inquire of me at all… I the Lord will answer him myself in keeping with his great idolatry, I will do this to recapture the hearts of the people of Israel who have all deserted me for their idols'" (Ezekiel 14:2-5).

58

We are all born sinners, in other words, idols-worshippers. An idol may not be a visible one; most of the time it is hidden in the heart, a secret imagination that takes the place of God. God is jealous. The most dangerous situation is when the blessings or gifts of God replace Him in the heart of the believer. Good things like marriage, ministry, anointing, worship, all these can become idols, 'wicked stumbling blocks,' when they become central to our lives.

One of the most difficult commands to obey is to love Jesus more than the members of your immediate family. It is hard to obey because the Word exposes your attachment to the secret idols of the heart. Jesus says that idolatry makes you 'unworthy' to represent Him as your Savior and Lord. Like a rejected vessel, not able to contain the new wine of the Spirit, this is the heart that loves another more than the Lord. Listen to these words: "anyone who loves his father or mother… his son or daughter more than me is not worthy of me…" (Matthew 10:37).

I remember the reaction I had when as baby Christian I read these words for the first time. Something strange rose inside me that said "this is not fair"; I knew my husband for more than ten years and I have known Jesus for only one month. How can I obey this command? I thought that it would be fair if I was to continue with the secret worship of my idol in my heart, which was my marriage. I thought that Jesus would accommodate Himself to it. I was wrong! Immediately I started defending my idol I discovered that I lost my peace and my joy. This was the first time when I knew what it means to grieve the Holy Spirit through hardness of heart. I was able to insist on my own way for only two days, I felt like dying, weak and sad beyond words. The third day I could not continue in rebellion and I confessed my sin, asking for forgiveness. I never felt so bad than when I realized that as a believer I can sin against the One who saved me. To the best of my knowledge, the sin against Love was the worst I have ever committed. Thank God I came back to the Cross and I never left since. I learned about the dangers of self-deception and spiritual wickedness and also the eternal value of the Cross in my life. "O, how I love Jesus…because He first loved me…"

In the scripture above (Ezekiel 14:2-5), we see a principle of God's judgment. Anyone who calls himself a believer and goes to God for prayer, for a request, or a prophet for guidance, God will answer according to that man's secret idol. In other words, God will permit deception to influence the mind of that man who prays and believes that his idol is a god after all. The purpose of God allowing this misleading in prayer is to expose the sin of idolatry, its shame and disappointment and at last to 'recapture the heart' of the backslider. This is how Jehovah God deals with hidden sin! It is a very painful process to be confronted by Truth, but this is the only way to freedom! The lesson is to pray first for God to expose the idols in the heart and we must be willing to repent of them. Then you will be free to ask for other blessings and prayer will be sweet to your soul.

"Search me, O God, and know my heart; test me and know my anxious thoughts. See if there is any offensive way in me and lead me in the way everlasting" (Psalm 139:23, 24).

UNFORGIVNESS

"And when you stand praying, if you hold anything against anyone, forgive him so that your father in heaven may forgive you" (Mark 11:25).

To forgive means to give up resentment or the claim for vengeance. It means that you let go of the idea that you are god to yourself. It means to trust God as the Judge of the earth. Therefore forgiveness is another form of faith in God, an expression of honor and worship of Christ who forgave His enemies on the cross (Luke 23:34; Ephesians 4:32). The simplest way to put it is: to choose between your pet vengeance and the answer to your prayer! You cannot hold on to both of them! I choose the privilege of prayer any time, any day!

WICKED GREED-IGNORING THE POOR

"Now this was the sin of your sister Sodom: She and her daughters were arrogant, overfed and unconcerned; they did not help the poor and the needy... therefore I did away with them as you have seen" (Ezekiel 16:49, 50).

"If a man shuts his ears to the cry of the poor he too will cry out and not be answered" (Proverbs 21:13).

God cares for the poor and the oppressed. He has commanded us to do the same. God is offended especially when we ignore the needy people but continue with religious activities. Do not show favoritism, do not discriminate those that are socially lower than you. See all people through the eyes of Christ who created them. Pride may be the reason why God ignores your prayers. Generosity and kindness to the poor is a sure open door to God in prayer.

DOUBT

"But when he asks, he must believe and not doubt because he who doubts is like the wave of the sea, blown and tossed by the wind. That man should not think he will receive anything from God; he is a double minded man, unstable in all he does" (James 1:6-8).

In the previous chapters, we have discussed about the sin of doubt. It means to hold to opposite opinions in the same time. It means to be too complicated spiritually; to say 'yes' and 'no' at the same time. Doubt is difficult to detect and can survive a long time in the heart undisturbed. Pray that God will open your eyes to see. Doubt closes the door to prayer and faith opens it.

ASKING AMISS-WRONG MOTIVES

"When you ask you do not receive because you ask with the wrong motives that you may spend on your pleasures" (James 4:3).

God looks and tests the heart. For Him, the motive of an action is more important than the action itself. We tend to be careless about the root of our problems and we desire to just have relief from them. God desires that we should pray for wisdom and for a pure heart that has the freedom to see and appreciate Him as a Person. God is holy and we are to be holy too. "Without holiness no one will see the Lord" or the value of prayer (Hebrews 12:14). A pure heart sees God when praying to Him (Matthew 5:8).

DIVISION IN MARRIAGE

"Wives, in the same way be submissive to your husbands... Husbands, in the same way be considerate with your wives and treat them with respect as the weaker partner and as heirs with you of the gracious gift of life, so that nothing will hinder your prayers" (1Peter3:1, 7).

Marriage is God's idea and plan for mankind. The devil hates it because of the unity of the Spirit between husband and wife, the platform for great answers to prayers (Matthew 18:19, 20). That is why God hates divorce; it breaks not only the human connection, but the covenant between them and God. Choose between a life of strife or a life of communion, worship, and prayer.

CHAPTER TEN

IMPORTANCE OF PRAYER

PRAY ALWAYS

"Then Jesus told his disciples a parable to show them that they should always pray and not give up... there was a widow in that town who kept coming to him with the plea: 'Grant me justice against my adversary'...will not God bring justice for his chosen ones who cry out to him day and night? Will he keep putting them off? I tell you, he will see that they get justice and quickly. However, when the Son of Man comes, will he find faith on the earth?"

~Luke 18: 1 - 8

We shall study the scriptures in Luke eighteen, from verses one to fourteen. Please read these slowly and prayerfully. Here we find the Lord talking to His disciples about the importance of prayer. The Word of God should be fresh to us every day. It is not how many scriptures you memorize; life is not a competition or a bible quiz. It is how much wisdom you have to apply the scriptures you know, with faith and patience, until you see results; visible fruit that gives glory to God alone. In answer to your prayers of faith there will be changes in your circumstances that can be attributed only to the work of the Holy Spirit. Amen!

God commands us to pray! In fact He commands us to pray 'always' with no interruptions, regardless of the circumstances. This simple command should be enough to reveal to us that God loves to hear His children talking to Him about all things. This command of praying always is a standard that God uses to measure faithfulness in His servants. You can never live a successful Christian life; you can never experience revival or breakthroughs, without praying faithfully for extended periods of time. The study of the Word of God and prayer are counted as major apostolic ministry that has the greatest reward (1 Thessalonians 5:17; Acts 6:4). Jesus says that we need faith and perseverance as we wait for God, who is not limited to any pattern or restriction of time when answering our prayers (1Thessalonians 5:17; Acts 6:4; Hebrews 6:12).

THE DANGER OF SPIRITUAL LAZINESS, FAINTING, OR GIVING UP THE PRIVILEDGE AND MINISTRY OF PRAYER!

Some prayers are answered immediately. Some are answered after a long time. As a general rule, we have a tendency to think that God is too slow in responding to our requests. It takes spiritual maturity to trust God without complaining for the timing and the modality of the answer to our prayer. The cross has done its deeps work and the heart has been circumcised by Christ for the man to remain joyful and grateful under the burden of yet unanswered prayers. The danger is that we get impatient, restless, lazy or passive spiritually; become deceived about the value of prayer and decide to stop it. This is called spiritual 'fainting,' a major hindrance to a successful prayer life. Once you chose to give up prayer, what is left is just wishful thinking that things may change one day. You lose the active faith to push forward and expect an answer to your request made long ago.

Let's look at the words 'to give up.' What does it mean? In Greek the words means to fail, to faint in the heart, to become weak and wicked, to harm yourself and others through doubt and rebellion. The same words mean to abandon an action because of the despair of success. The man becomes a coward; he fails and betrays his destiny when he estimates that the miracle has become impossible even for God to perform. For example, he chooses to believe that the sickness is incurable and God is not available or able to heal his body. He accepts and declares defeat without waiting for the final hour when God judges and rewards according to each man's work. This spiritual fainting is worldly sorrow and a symbol of death. By choosing to stop prayer, a man abandons the desire to see a miraculous change in his circumstances and he aborts his dream. The choice to stop prayer is the silent but sure signal of backsliding. Selah!

We see that 'to give up' means to surrender to failure, to discontinue a good work or to resign. It is a matter of control. Like the man who commits suicide just to prove that he is in charge of his life. Spiritually speaking, it means to deliberately choose to allow the enemy to take over your position of standing before the throne. You surrender your blessing of communion with God to another with no possibility of resuming it in the future. What a tragedy to stop the prayer of faith! What great loss!

The opposite is to hold on, to abide, to dwell in the same place of waiting without interruptions. In other words, pray until something happens ('PUSH'). It is a great dishonor to God to give up prayer because of circumstances that look contrary to the expected miracle. This is a great revelation! The devil does not care if we start a prayer request; he does not care if we join the line of waiting before the throne. But later he comes to persuade us that we have waited too long and he offers himself to stand in our place. Satan is a thief and a fake 'intercessor.' He desires to take over your place of blessings!

Be careful! The pressure from the enemy will increase as you get closer to the moment when the prayer will be manifested in the natural realm. Then pray like the widow: "Lord – grant me justice against my adversary!" Pray for the justice of your cause as you continue to give glory to God! Jesus is giving us a warning here not to be fools. Do not abandon the place of waiting which will eventually become the place of testimony, blessing and miracles! Selah!

THE FAITHFUL, PATIENT WOMAN – REWARDED AND FULFILLED – JOY AT LAST

Let us look closely at Luke eighteen verses one through eight; in this parable Jesus introduces us to a woman who is in great need. Let's identify with her and we shall only gain. The first thing we are told about her is that she is a widow. She has no human helper. The trust in man is cursed by God. There are people that say that they do not trust anybody, but they trust themselves. That will end in disappointment and failure. The result of this misplaced trust is a spiritual blindness and bareness, a lonely isolated soul. Repent and turn your heart towards God. Have faith in God alone and you will never be put to shame. God will position you in a 'watered' place where you will be fruitful and a blessing to many. The result of this blessed life is that you will be free from any fears that the natural man experiences. This holy assurance is a sign that your faith is in God alone (Jeremiah 17:5-8).

Let's go back to our 'sister,' the widow. She is poor, lonely and troubled. She has an enemy who knows she is vulnerable and weak. The enemy takes advantage of that and persecutes her continuously. She is the picture of the true believer. The attacks from the devil are strong and unfair. For a long time she can only cry for 'justice from the adversary.' She does not take the matter into her own hands, but goes to the official judge who alone has the authority to help. Her situation is made difficult by the fact that the judge is a hard person, with no respect for God or man.

She wisely recognizes the fact that all authority comes from God (Romans 13:1-5). It does not matter if the official, the leader, is a kind person or not. It does not matter if he is willing to attend to her case or not. She is too poor to bribe him; her poverty is strength because she has nothing to lose and no fear from the enemy. She knows that God is in charge of all situations on earth and He will answer them that have faith and cry to Him 'day and night.' This is a stumbling block to rebellious and proud people. They do not acknowledge the sovereignty of God who delegates His authority to whom He wants, to saints or sinners alike (Daniel 5:21). It is God that has the last say in all human affairs. You should know that it does not matter if the leader, the boss or the judge is good or bad to you. God is in charge! I am a believer and God is on my case! If God says 'yes' no man can say 'no'! This 'little' secret is the foundation of a successful Christian life! God is in charge of His creation and God answers the prayers of His people! The Almighty God is your Father! That is all you need to know! Amen!

Please note that this woman has only one option to escape the torment of the enemy: the weapon of prayer. It may not look like much, but prayer is the greatest power given to man. The old saints said it like this: "Prayer moves the hand that moves the mountains." Believing prayer can never be entertainment; it can never be just a form of useless talking to an imaginary being. Prayer is communion and worship between a child of God and the Father. God invented prayer and He promised to listen to it. You need to have faith that it is so! 'The prayer of the upright pleases God... He hears the prayer of the righteous" (Proverbs 15:8, 29). The widow identified the judge as God's delegated authority and then she made her choice: for as long as she is alive, she will continue to come with her petition; she will not be tired or discouraged by anything she sees or hears in the court house. She decided that she will come until her case is solved, until she is declared free from the torment of her enemy. This was her secret. This is the secret of answers to prayers.

The effect of the spirit of religion upon the churches is that for many, prayer is just 'an activity' expected from a Christian. People pray, but not from faith. They just pray hoping that it may achieve some result. That is prayer of doubt. 'Trial by error' type of prayer is doubt based. God has promised to ignore any communication that proceeds from doubt (James 1:6-8). Just adding the name of Jesus at the end of a petition will not change the fact that it proceeds from doubt. It is a rejected prayer. The lesson here is this: examine your heart and search to see if true faith in God is resident there. If the answer is 'yes,' then your prayer will always be answered by God, sooner or later! This is God's promise! This is so simple, even a child can understand it. Meditate on this: God always answers prayers of faith and perseverance!

THE PROUD RELIGIOUS ENEMY – DEFEATED AND DISAPPOINTED BY THE WOMAN'S FAITH AND PERSEVERANCE

The Lord then goes on and tells them another parable. It is about two men who go to the Temple to pray. Because these two parables are found together in the same chapter, possibly during the same speech, I believe that they are connected. That is why we should pay attention to them. In these two parables is found a description of the One who judges all prayers. The first man is rich, successful, and obviously religious. He looks like an elder in the church. He prays about and for himself. He compares himself with others, confident that he is better. He is a proud, religious unbeliever, ignorant of how much God hates his sin.

He may represent the enemy of the widow who persecutes her. To him, she is a foolish woman who God did not bless enough, because her husband died and left her alone. Maybe he was trying to seduce her. He was possibly a friend to the unkind judge so he was sure that the widow had no place to escape from his pressure. Proud people always ignore the God 'factor.' They do not believe that God is interested in helping the helpless who pray for mercy and grace at His Throne.

Please see the danger of doubt coming from the spirit of religion through men who attend church. This evil spirit will tell you that you are wasting your time praying; that you do not need to pay the price to seek and find Jesus, the Author and Finisher of true faith in God; that you are too insignificant to the God of the Universe and that He does not know you; that you should abandon the holy place of prayer and do something more 'practical' than that.

God judges the proud by refusing to justify them, to give them peace or to answer their prayers. God is the Rock of defense and the Avenger of them that put their trust in Him. Woman, you who pray for the salvation of your husband or children… You barren woman who pray to receive the fruit of the womb… You single woman who desire the gift of marriage… You who are sick in the body and mind, persecuted and lonely…PRAY AND HAVE FAITH IN GOD! God is never too early and never too late. He has heard your cries and has seen your tears. He will surely come and rescue you from this heavy burden that no man can carry. He will come to give you the testimony of victory and of a changed life! To the glory and honor of the name of Jesus Christ!

"Imitate those who thru faith and patience inherit what has been promised" (Hebrews 6:12). Amen!

CHAPTER ELEVEN

THE LORD'S PRAYER

A RICH PATTERN TO FOLLOW

"This then is how you should pray: Our Father in heaven, hallowed be your name…"
~Matthew 6: 9

I have been waiting patiently to come back to the Book of Matthew, chapter six. Here we have what is called the Lord's Prayer. When the disciples saw Jesus praying, there was something strange, attractive and beautiful about it. Possibly they thought that there is 'a secret key' to successful prayer life. Whatever may have been the reason for asking how to pray, it was a blessed request because we now have in the Word of God the pattern of prayer given by none other than our Lord. There are many books written about this subject. Many saints in the past have received revelations on how to improve their communion with God. I will limit myself to what I found as I study the Word of God. One thing for sure: Jesus commands us to pray! This should be enough for us! "You should pray…" (Matthew 6:9).

Our Father in Heaven

The first thing I see is that this is a pattern of prayer and not just a prayer itself. People have memorized the verses and recite it as a poem. It is beautiful, no doubt, but there is something deeper than what our eyes see on the surface. We shall address now the first two words. They are addressed to God the Father whose dwelling place is in heaven.

Prayer is a personal relationship, communion and discourse between the believer on earth and his Father in heaven. Prayer is not just talking

69

religious things or making some requests to God. Prayer is a bridge of life between two spirits: one on earth and God in heaven.

Prayer is a very strong exercise because it has to unite two very different persons who live very far from one another. Man is born in sin and God hates sin. Outside the exercise of prayer done in the name of Jesus, no man can approach God at all. Heaven is the place where God dwells, in a way He does not do so outside that realm. Heaven is also the place where God has established His throne for judgment. It is the place where the glory of God, the beauty of His holiness is its very atmosphere. In heaven the Name of God is exalted and the Word of God is settled forever (Psalm 9:7; 11:4; 119:89; 148:13).

THE FIRST STEP IN PRAYER IS WORSHIP

All true prayer starts with thoughts of God, Our Father in heaven. All fake prayer starts with thoughts of us and our needs. We are commanded to 'go boldly' and 'with confidence' before the throne of God 'in our time of need' (Hebrews 4:16). Boldly does not mean rudely. It means to be free to speak from your heart. But we are to pause a little, take a breath and remind ourselves that we are going before God Almighty. No matter how important we think our needs are, we bow before God Almighty. This is the first step of prayer.

We know that there is great distance between man on earth and God in heaven. Naturally speaking, there is no connection at all. Prayer is totally impossible from the realm of the flesh. I say this so that we can appreciate the wonder and privilege of prayer. Prayer is addressed to God the Father. It is a family business. No religious believer can address God as 'Father.' If he tries to pray the best he can say is: 'Our Creator in heaven...'

THE DEVIL IS THE FATHER OF LIES

I read somewhere that the Pharisees did not regard God as their father. That is why they hated Jesus so much because he told them that God is His Father (Matthew 5:18). If you are in Christ, you will suffer the same persecution of rejection from religious spirits in the church. They will think that you are presumptuous and will reject you for that. The religious hypocrites have a different father and he is the devil (John 8:44). They are trained to lie, 'kill, steal and destroy'; to persecute believers and to mock at the saints. But 'wisdom is justified by her children' (Matthew 11:19, KJ). I am really amazed at God! He calls me His child! This is beyond any of my childhood imagination! O...the Blood of Jesus...

PRAYER IS INTIMATE COMMUNION WITH THE FATHER

Prayer is an intimate discussion with our Father. God is God to all His creation, but He is Father only to them that are born again, to them that have the Holy Spirit of Adoption and belong to Christ. These words remind us that we should be 'in the Spirit' when we approach God. The word Father is intimate. The prayer is intimate, but not selfish. Jesus does not say we should address God as 'My Father.' It is 'Our Father.' I have to remind myself that I belong to a big family and others have needs too and pray to Him as well. They that pray will become lovers of God and of one another in the body of Christ. People that pray together love one another. This is especially true in the home. The husband and wife that pray together will love one another with the supernatural love of Christ.

FEAR GOD WHEN YOU PRAY

Please take note that we should never take God for granted. We are to be intimate with Him in prayer, but never over-familiar. The fear of God is the beginning of wisdom and knowledge in prayer (Proverbs 1:7).

"Guard your steps when you go to the house of God... Do not be quick with your mouth, do not be hasty in your heart to utter anything before God. God is in heaven and you are on earth so let your words be few..." (Ecclesiastes 5:1, 2).

We should have a holy respect for God. We are told to prepare our hearts and mouths before we pray. God has nothing to lose. But we can grieve the Holy Spirit through improper protocol. We can lose fellowship with the Holy Spirit and that is a great sin and loss indeed that needs confession and repentance from the heart.

OUR PRAYERS PASS THROUGH THE AIR TO HEAVEN

Our prayers are heard by God because of the intercession of Jesus, our High Priest. He died on the cross, was buried, and resurrected on the third day. After forty days He ascended to heaven against the law of gravity. The 'ruler of the kingdom of the air,' the devil, could not stop Jesus who had 'gone through the heavens' back to the Father (Ephesians 2:2, 2: Hebrews 4:14). This is very important to remember. Our prayers pass through the passage in the air left open for us by the Son of God. If I believe that Jesus went back to heaven, then I should believe that my prayers will reach the Father and will be answered by Him. Amen!

THE TRUTH ABOUT GOD THE FATHER AND PRAYER

In the book of Matthew chapter six, the words 'Father in heaven' appear 12 times. Gleaning the revelation from here we make the following observations:

- I have a Father. I am not an orphan or a bastard. I belong to the greatest family in the universe.
- My Father is God Almighty.
- My Father lives far away in a place called Heaven, where He is the King of all.
- My Father loves, welcomes, and patiently waits for me to come to Him in prayer.
- My Father sees me. His eyes are upon me always directing me with His graze. I can never hide from Him.
- I cannot see my Father except I go to His presence, in the Spirit, to 'the secret place of the Most High God.'
- I have to pay the price to go and see and talk to my Father. Prayer is sacrifice and privilege at the same time.
- If I am in flesh, I cannot please or find God in prayer (Romans 8:8). I need to die to the flesh and to sin so that I can pray well.
- Pleasing men with my religious activities is living in flesh. I choose to hide from the eyes, applause, and rewards of men.

- My Father is generous and rewards me with Himself. This is the highest reward in the Universe.
- My Father and I become one in prayer. Each prayer makes me stronger so I will pray more not less.
- My Father commands me to pray. I have to obey. Obedience means life and worship and more prayer (John 14:21).
- My Father knows all things, even the things and desires of my heart. But He still wants me to pray.
- My Father waits for me to meet Him in prayer and worship. I will not let God wait too long for me. I will pray always!
- My Father forgives my sins for the sake of His Son Jesus Christ. I am grateful that I can pray.
- My Father expects me to do the same and forgive others, so that I will be like Him. Prayer will be sweeter because we are one!
- My Father is the most generous, loving, and gracious Person in the Universe. He feeds all creation. No need to fear, but pray.

All these statements are based on the Word of God which is Truth. The truth has to be in me, by feeding daily on the Word of God. Prayer is God's idea and not mine. To pray means I obey God and His protocol of meeting with Him. I need to have faith that God waits for me to pray. He will edit my prayers if need be and answer them. I should never think that prayer is a burden or the activity of a fool. When invited to a prayer meeting in my church, my spirit and soul should be excited and happy. This should be the normal lifestyle for me. If I refuse to pray it means that I reject my identity and my place in the family of God. I will become isolated and vulnerable to the attacks of the enemy. So I choose to pray without ceasing, with passion and faith. I should never be tired of prayer. Amen!

Jesus is not just teaching us about prayer. His life and death is our example and pattern. He lived and died in the presence of God the Father. He did all things to please the Father. The secret of Jesus was that He and the Father are one. This spiritual unity is the secret foundation for successful prayer life. When Jesus was just twelve he stayed behind in the temple He called 'My Father's House.' His last prayers on the cross were addressed to the Father. "Father forgive them… Father into your hands I commit my spirit" (Luke 2:49; 23:34, 46).

Prayer has a life of its own. No one can teach me prayer if I refuse to pray. It is not just theory, not just a Bible study or a doctrine. It is my lifeline with my Father and my own identity in Him. I should accept the fact that stopping to pray is sin and suicide. Prayer is a fruit out of real communion with God. I cannot learn how to pray successfully, but in the same time refuse to live like Jesus or to be disobedient to His word. God cannot be manipulated. Conditions have to be fulfilled before rewards are given. This is a spiritual law that none can break.

Finally, prayer is comfort. Each prayer reminds me that I belong to someone, to a family, and that I can never be alone. Each prayer is an exchange of whispers of love and kisses of trust that takes me out from this ordinary life into the Spirit that knows no end. During prayer I stretch my wings of faith to fly, to touch the rainbow of peace above the dark clouds of the storm. I see the door open, I hear the future sing, I dance to the melody of strings in heaven and I embrace the Amen. This is my prayer…

"This is then, is how you should pray: Our Father in heaven, hallowed be your name…" (Matthew 6:9).

We shall focus our attention on the words: 'HALLOWED BE YOUR NAME.'

The word 'hallowed' in both Hebrew and Greek means to be or to make holy, consecrated, blameless and pure. Whatever is hallowed is separated from the common use of men and completely dedicated to God. This separation from the world has only one purpose: God alone will use it, for His glory and pleasure. It is God's portion, prepared for His honor. Anyone that defiles a holy thing will be punished by God whose name is jealous. Other things declared holy are the Sabbath, the priests and their garments, the anointing oil, the offerings, and the Temple in general.

The word 'name' in Hebrew means a definite, conspicuous, position of authority, of fame and public honor. The name of God cannot be ignored or hidden in the darkness. It is always accompanied by loud praise and worship, giving glory to Him alone. Heaven is a holy place. God's name is proclaimed as holy in heaven and it should be the same on earth.

The study of the names of God in the Bible is too big for any man to finish. We shall discuss here some basics about the meaning and power of God's name. The more revelation we have, the more we shall be able to 'hallow' His name and pray. The name of God is not just a word. God has revealed Himself, His character and Person, through His names. Starting with the first name: Elohim, in Genesis 1:1, God reveals Himself to us, gradually adding fresh revelation to what we know about Him. May we desire to come closer to God and understand His Names and His Person! May we desire to pray more than ever before!

Hallowed be Your Name

"Hallowed be your name..."
~Matthew 6: 9

- Elohim (The Creator of heaven and earth) – Genesis 1:1
- Jehovah (I AM, the absolutely self-existent one) – Genesis 2:4
- Elyon (The Most High God; the one that enters the battle and always wins) Genesis 14
- Adonai (The Master, the Lord and the Owner of all slaves) – Genesis15
- EL Shaddai (The powerful One, the Giver of Miracles, of new beginnings and revival) –Genesis 17
- Jehovah Jireh (The Provider of the Substitute) –Genesis 22
- Jehovah Rapha (The Healer) –Exodus 15
- Jehovah Nissi (The Banner Lifted High in Victory) - Exodus 17
- El Quanna (Jealous) –Exodus 34
- Jehovah Kaddash (The Sanctifier) –Leviticus 20
- Jehovah Shalom (Our Peace) –Judges
- The Lord of Hosts (The Commander of the Armies of Angels and Saints) 1 Samuel 17:45
- Jehovah Rohi (Our Shepherd) –Psalm 23
- Wonderful Counselor –Isaiah 7
- Everlasting Father –Isaiah 9:6
- Immanuel (God is with us) –Isaiah 7
- Jehovah Tsidkenu (Our Righteousness) –Jeremiah 23
- Jehovah Shammah (The Presence) –Ezra 48:35
- The Messiah (The Anointed One and His Anointing; the Christ) –Daniel 9:25, 26
- Jesus Christ
- The HOLY SPIRIT (The Spirit of Truth, the Gift of the Father, the Spirit of life and peace)

HOW TO HALLOW GOD'S NAME

- PRAISE AND HONOR GOD'S NAME ALWAYS!

"You shall not take the name of the Lord your God in vain, for the Lord will not hold him guiltless who takes his name in vain" (Exodus 20:7; NKJ).

To obey God's third commandment means to refuse to associate God's name with sin or with anything that does not bring Him glory. It also means to be careful not to associate the name of Jesus with selfish prayers. We should call His name when we are in need, with worship and faith! This is the only commandment that has a warning of punishment if broken. In Hebrew, the word 'in vain' means something deceptive, evil, idolatry, useless, of no effect. The lesson here is that we should either call God's name in times of need, with faith and honor, or we should not pray at all.

"...sing praise to his name; extol him who rides on the clouds; his name is the Lord- and rejoice before him!"(Psalm 68:4).

Each revelation of God's name and character should produce the desire to praise Him. This desire to sing, to worship God's name is the root of our joy in His presence. It is a privilege to know, to meditate on God's name and on His great acts of power.

"I am the Lord; that is my name! I will not give my glory to another or my praise to idols. See, the former things have taken place and new things I declare; before they spring into being, I announce them to you" (Isaiah 42:8, 9).

The devil stained the name and the character of God when he deceived Adam and Eve and they disobeyed. Since the fall of man, the praise, honor and glory due God's name were marred. Jesus came not only to reveal the Father to us, but to restore the glory and praise of His name. These 'new things' prophesied by God Himself is the coming of Christ amongst men, His life and death on the cross. He sent the Holy Spirit through whom we can now pray and hallow the name of the Father.

- BE HAPPY WHEN YOU CALL GOD'S NAME

"Pleasing is the fragrance of your perfumes; your name is like perfume poured out. No wonder the maidens love you!" (Song of Songs 1:3)

The name of the Lord is like perfume, attractive, pleasing, strong enough to change all that come in contact with. Like Mary's alabaster box, broken to anoint Jesus before His death, so the name of the Lord spoken in faith penetrates through all hearts. "And the house was filled with the fragrance of the perfume (John 12:3). Like the fragrance of Christ, His name is most powerful. It gives life to the humble, but it kills the proud. The name of the Lord is like burning incense, the sign and seal of victory in heaven and on earth (2 Corinthians 2:14-16).

- WHEN CALLING GOD'S NAME BELIEVE IN MIRACLES

"Those who know your name will trust in you, for you, Lord, have never forsaken those who seek you" (Psalm 9:10). "In the name of Jesus Christ of Nazareth, walk!" (Acts 3:6)

The reward for us as we study God's names is an increased faith in Him and the power to believe in miracles. The religious hypocrites will persecute you, but they cannot take your revelations or your miracles (Acts 3 and 4).

- GOD'S NAME IS PROTECTION TO HIS CHILDREN

"May the name of the God of Jacob protect you" (Psalm 20:1).

The word 'protect' in Hebrew means to be lifted up, to make you so high that your enemies cannot reach you. The name of the Lord spoken in faith is victory; it is promotion for you, a going to a higher level of anointing spiritual; (Psalm 91:14).

This protection is only for the children of God who run in faith towards the name in time of trouble. They identify with God's Word, become one with Him, until they 'disappear' into the Strong Tower of His blessed name (Proverbs 18:10).

If you dishonor the name of God in times of 'peace' you will not be able 'to run' and locate it for protection in times of trouble.

- LEARN TO USE THE NAME OF GOD IN WARFARE

David confronted the giant and won the victory with faith in the Word and in the Name of God:

"You come against me with sword and spear and javelin, but I come against you in the Name of the Lord Almighty, the God of the armies of Israel, whom you have defied...for the battle is the Lord's" (1 Samuel 17:45, 47).

This is a very important principle. The owner of the weapons, of the battle itself and of the final result is God. It is very useful to study the names of God. It is like sharpening the sword that knows no defeat. Every minute you dedicate to Bible study and prayer increases your discernment and your strength in warfare.

God cannot lose any battle. Jesus has defeated all the powers of darkness at the cross. His name "Jesus Christ" and also faith in His name is enough for us to apply His victory to daily challenges. It is not magic. It is the Sword of the Spirit, the Word of God and the name of God spoken with faith. It is the fullness and maturity of the believer in Christ that predicts the winner in the battle.

"The horse is made ready for the day of battle but the victory rests with the Lord" (Proverbs 21:31).

- TRUST GOD FOR THE UNITY OF THE SPIRIT IN
  PRAYER PRODUCED BY HIS NAME

"Again I tell you that if two of you on earth agree about anything you ask, it will be done for you by my Father in heaven. For where two or three come together in my name, there am I with them." (Matthew 18:19, 20)

The words 'come together' are very powerful. They describe an organic union, alive and strong, a true spiritual bond that is complete and mature. The two or three coming together, represent life at the conception stage. The gathering is so small, the bond is spiritual, invisible to the human eye, and yet, that is the beginning of the spiritual pregnancy. The name of Jesus produces life in the believer and in the body of Christ. This is the perfect environment for acceptable prayer and worship.

In conclusion: for as long as you remain ignorant of the power, the honor, and glory reserved for God alone, you are still in bondage to the devil. I beseech you to pay the price and study God's Word, especially to know God's names and character. That is the proof that you are free from sin, a child of God indeed! Then you can pray: 'Heavenly Father, hallowed be your name!"

Pray Ye

Your Kingdom come, Your will be done on Earth as it is in Heaven

"Your kingdom come, your will be done on earth as it is in heaven"
~Matthew 6: 10

We shall continue with the study of the pattern of prayer taught by the Lord. We have looked at the way we should enter the presence of God, recognizing that He is our Father in Heaven. Then we saw the value and power of identifying with the Name of God, the Name of Jesus! This revelation is sufficient to make our hearts tremble!

Now we shall look at the meaning of the Kingdom, of God and at the privilege the believers have as citizens of heaven. Prayer is the communication network, the language of the Kingdom of God and worship is its atmosphere.

A kingdom on earth is a territory that is ruled by a king or a queen. A monarch inherits his title, has the highest office in the land and rules for life. The Kingdom of God is an invisible territory, a spiritual country whose capital is heaven and whose King is God. The citizens of heaven are scattered all over the world and they are called the children of God. They have different languages and skin colors, some are rich and some are poor in earthly goods, but they all have one thing in common; they are family. They are born again by the Spirit and Water and they have the same Father and God. These people have become united by the baptism of the Holy Spirit who connects them into one Body of Christ. Jesus says that the Kingdom of God manifested on earth is made up of a mixed multitude. The visible church contains also religious people that are not of God. Just like the wheat and the weeds grow together in the field, together but not united, so there is a mixture of people in the church. They all profess to serve the same King. They all pray and claim to go to heaven. That is the visible Kingdom of God, much bigger than the real, spiritual one. The Kingdom is a mystery; it is not easy to describe it. Jesus used parables and stories to help us to understand it. A parable Jesus told are simple earthly story that has a heavenly meaning. Jesus said often; "The Kingdom of God is like…"

THE KINGDOM OF GOD IS INVISIBLE, BUT REAL

"Jesus declared: "I tell you the truth, no one can see the Kingdom of God unless he is born again" (John 3:3).

God made it in such a way that the spiritual realities are hidden from the eyes of the natural man. The kingdom of God is a treasure indeed, beyond any words to describe its value. But this treasure is hidden in a field or like an expensive pearl, in the deep of the sea (Matthew 13:44-46). The blessings of God do not lie on the surface of the ground.

God does not reveal the blessed secrets of His Kingdom to the careless, superficial religious men. Jesus is the King of kings in His Kingdom. The entrance in the Kingdom is possible only by His Spirit. To the natural man all spiritual things are foolishness; he does not understand and has no interest in knowing them (1 Corinthians 2:14). This ignorance is dangerous because the Spirit realm is a reality: "Righteousness, peace and joy in the Holy Ghost" (Romans14:17).

The Bible is the constitution of the Kingdom of God. To the natural man even the Bible looks foolish. He can only read it as a story book and not as the Word of Life. To the unbeliever all things that cannot be touched with the hand, cannot be seen with the eyes, cannot be heard with the ears, all these are nonexistent. I know this because for more than thirty years of my life I was an atheist. I did not believe in the existence of God or His Kingdom. I remember that for me, heaven and hell where pure imagination. God and the devil did not exist except in the minds of religious, illiterate people. Looking back, I see how foolish I was. Thank God for His mercy to me.

Pray: "Lord Jesus, open my eyes that I may see You and Your Kingdom!"

THE KINGDOM OF GOD HAS TO BE SOUGHT

"But seek first the kingdom and his righteousness and all these things will be given to you as well" (Matthew 6:33).

You have to seek until you find the blessings. It is never easy! The word 'seek' means to go in search for, to try to discover, to buy, or gain something that you desire. To seek requires a clear vision and concentrated effort. You need to have holy curiosity, a sense of adventure, and boldness to take necessary risk. You cannot be intimidated by failure, by cover up. You need to explore possible places of concealment. It means to leave comfort behind and move ahead searching, asking, and looking. You must value the hidden thing; you should not be satisfied with the surface or the package, even if it's beautiful to human eyes. The opposite of seeking diligently to find your blessings is that you will feel poor and unfulfilled. In the absence of the blessed content, you will only find power hidden in a wrap of weakness, or treasures buried in cheap plastic bags.

If you are the person that seeks God's Kingdom first: You seek God 'early' (Psalm 63:1) like a dying man, desperate for a purpose in life. You go to sleep, tired and afraid that you will die an untimely death, like Jacob, with God as your pillow. You dream about God walking with you in the garden of spices. You wake up with God early in the morning, longing for a whisper of love and a drop of hope that He knows you by name. You encourage yourself to seek God trusting the promise that the effort is not in vain. You see many fields; some with green grass; some with flowers in bloom. But you continue to search for that field that has a well of oil beneath, fed from the deep heart of God. Your eyes get used to seeing in the shadows, to scan under the dry leaves of autumn. Still asking, still seeking..." Have you seen the One my heart loves?" (Songs of Songs 3:3).

The world laughs at people who seek God. For the world, they are useless, double fools. But this is the secret and this is the power. But at last, when all is spent and gone, you become the landlord of a piece of heaven on earth, a treasure that keeps your heart on fire for the Giver of Gifts, an eternal victory that can never be lost.

I can't teach you how to seek God. There is no formula given to man. You have to do it by yourself; cry your own tears; wait and waste your own time, not mine. But one thing I guarantee you: the treasure called Christ and His Kingdom is more than all you have seen, heard or imagine; and yes, you will live with Him happily ever after! All riches follow him who seeks God with all his heart. So, start praying all manner of prayers! It is better to pray more than less! Read the Word! Believe the Word! Praise God and Christ! And the door will be open to you!

81

THE KINGDOM OF GOD IS FOR SINNERS WHO REPENT

The first message preached by John the Baptist and by the Lord was this: "Repent, for the Kingdom of God is near" (Matthew 3:2; 4:17). The word 'repent' means to have a change of mind concerning the sin of unbelief in particular. True repentance and conversion is the peculiar work of the Holy Spirit. The natural man cannot repent because he does not see the need for it. He is proud, satisfied with his mind as it is and has no desire to change it.

The beginning of true conversion starts with the coming of the Holy Spirit on you, to convict you of sin (John 16:8-11). Suddenly you feel bad about doubting the Word of God; you start feeling guilty about taking the name of God in vain. You start thinking about God, about death and the judgment that follows. All these manifest as a form of depression; you begin to hate the pleasures of sin. It is a strange new feeling you never had before. Eventually you are led to make a choice and surrender your life to the Lord. Coming to the Cross with your sin, asking for forgiveness and mercy…this is the most painful event in the life of a sinner, like his dying song, it is called repentance. The end of it is peace with God, the joy of salvation, the entrance into the Kingdom of God as son or daughter. There is no other way to enter the Kingdom except you are born again by the Spirit of God.

I want to add something here: There is a danger of experiencing a religious 'conversion' brought about by a desire to be a member of a church. The root of it is the evil spirit of religion who convinces many that just going to church and participating in activities is enough to be called a believer and to go to heaven. Just be aware of this danger when witnessing to others. Do not put unnecessary pressure on anyone to be 'saved.' Lead them to the cross. Pray that the Holy Spirit will do His work in them. Let repentance be real. Let them pray with their own words. Let them weep if necessary. Let God be God to them. Then salvation will be true and their joy will be real.

THE KINGDOM OF GOD IS POWERFUL AND ETERNAL

Isaiah prophesied that the Messiah will come and… "of the increase of his government and peace there shall be no end" (Isaiah 9:7). God revealed to Daniel that the rock cut out without human hands will completely destroy the idol image. Then the rock itself will grow to become a great mountain, a kingdom that will be given to the people of God forever (Daniel 2:34-45). God reveals to Mary that her son Jesus will be the greatest King and "He will reign over the house of Jacob forever; His kingdom will never end" (Luke 1:32, 33). All prayers and worship should rest on the confidence that salvation is real and eternal, the gift of God, given by grace alone.

Jesus said that the Kingdom of God starts like a small mustard seed planted in good soil. When it grows it is a big tree (Matthew 13:31, 32). Never despise the days of 'little things' in the Spirit realm (Zechariah 4:10). The Kingdom of God has the greatest potential in the whole universe to beat all odds and to grow, mature, and become fruitful. Believe that!

The will of God in heaven is simply this: To worship God, and King Jesus; the Lamb upon the throne! There is no hindrance to this eternal worship. The devil wanted to stop it, to steal some of the glory. But he failed! He was cast down on earth and at last he will be destroyed in the eternal lake of fire (See Revelation 20). All prayer and all worship in the Kingdom of God must flow from the grateful hearts of the redeemed. To obey the command "Pray without ceasing" is the proof that the will of God is done among us as it is already done in heaven. Let earth imitate heaven! Let prayer flow like a river of life going up "… the mountain that rises above the hills and all nations will stream to it" (Isaiah 2:2). Let worship rise freely from earth to supply our High Priest with incense for His eternal glory! Amen!

Give us today our daily bread

"Give us today our daily bread..."
~Matthew 6: 11

PRAYER FOR PROVISION

Thus far we've learned how 'to pause' in order that we may worship Him, whose name is Holy. We now have His 'ear' and we can proceed to the second 'step' of prayer: making personal requests.

This is a simple but very important lesson: except for the occasional 'emergency,' do not come before God with a 'prayer list' of things you desire to receive. You worship God first of all. You dwell in His presence, just like a father and son visiting together. Do not manipulate His anointing. Do not be impatient to talk. "Go near to listen rather than to offer sacrifice of fools... Do not be in a hurry to leave the Kings presence..." (Ecclesiastes 5:1: 8:3). Listen to God who is talking to you, revealing things unknown to you before. Thank God for the opportunity to call Him. Prayer is a privilege!

We shall study the sentence above: "Give us today our daily bread..." it is made up of six words and each is important. The first thing we discover is that we are supposed to ask our Father for the provision of our spiritual and material needs. The request is in particular for bread to eat. This may sound strange to our ears. Most people do not think of God; they do not bother to ask Him for food, for bread. This is because we are rebellious and independent by nature. We just assume that food is our right or the product of our labor. A man calls himself 'the Bread Winner' of his family. If he is religious, he may pray to eat some fancy, expensive food, but rarely does he remember to pray for 'ordinary' bread. He forgets that it is God 'who gives bread to the eater' (See Isaiah 55:10). Except for the homeless, it is very rare that a man prays for a loaf of bread. We see here that the Lord teaches us humility and simplicity in life.

In most cultures, bread is still the basic and the cheapest food. If you eat bread, you can never be hungry. We are not told to ask for cake, fried chicken, or salad. Just ask for bread and be satisfied with bread. The lesson is that if we have to take Jesus seriously, it means that from today, each time I see a slice of bread, I should immediately remember my Father in heaven. The opposite is that if I eat without thinking of God, without praying and giving thanks for my food, it means that I am a thief. By taking the bread on the table for granted I am in danger of losing all my property (Proverbs 6:30, 32). Selah!

Like the beautiful rainbow reminds me of peace, like the mountains remind me of strength, like a river in the desert gives me hope to live, so even a crust of bread should make me to worship our Father in heaven, Jehovah Jireh, God the Provider. We are to ask for 'daily bread'; a holy habit of prayer and trust. It is not weekly or monthly; it is not supposed to be done just occasionally, when we feel 'religious.' The request is to be for enough bread to feed all who depend on us. I should never use my faith or my 'skill' of prayer for selfish purposes. I pray for 'OUR bread,' not for 'MY bread.' Not all people pray or trust God for their provision of food. My faith has to grow; my heart has to accommodate others, friends and even enemies, who depend on me at the table. The daily provision of bread on the table may be the weapon of warfare I was waiting for. "If your enemy is hungry, feed him... in doing this you will heap burning coals on his head... Overcome evil with good" (Romans 12:20, 21). I have won many battles at my kitchen table just from the revelation of bread as a weapon. Selah!

OUR HUNGER

There is much revelation about the way God feeds His creation. "Look at the birds of the air... your heavenly Father feeds them" (Matthew 6:26). Just think of it: every animal, bird, and fish, big or small, they are all fed by God!

In the desert, the people of God experienced hunger. We are told that the need for food was sent by God to humble them, to force them to come to God and pray. Some people prayed but most of them failed the test of faith and grumbled when hungry. "He humbled you causing you to hunger and then feeding you with manna which you nor your fathers had known, to teach you that man does not live on bread alone but on every word that comes from the mouth of the Lord" (Deuteronomy 8:3). God does nothing without a purpose. God sends hunger to humble us so that He can bless us. A truly humble man is one who ranks himself low in the social status. He has renounced fame, luxuries and power over others. He lives in total dependence on God, trusting that He will provide for all his needs. Humility is the fruit of the Holy Spirit in the child of God. No unbeliever can ever be humble. He may display a false, religious humility but in his heart he is proud and independent of God. The true humble people are blessed by God with favor, happiness, peace and joy. They dwell in the revelation of Christ as their personal friend. "Blessed are those who hunger… for righteousness for they will be filled… God gives grace to the humble" (Matthew 6:6, 1 Peter 5:5).

The prodigal son was happy in the strange land of sin until the famine came and 'he began to be in need.' His new job required him to feed the pigs, but he could not share in their food. The hunger was the lowest point in his life. He remembered the food in his father's house; even the servants had more than enough. That is when 'he came to his senses,' turned his back to sin and came back home, to his father's house (Luke 15:11-32). Don't forget: Hunger is a friend sent by God!

But there is another element to it. God sends famine on a territory as a sign of judgment that requires national repentance. Joseph became Prime Minister of Egypt because he understood the purpose of the famine sent by God and had the revelation of the solution to it. A famine sent by God is a more powerful weapon than the sword or the plague (Jeremiah 24:10). The system of this world will be destroyed suddenly by a deadly famine. No business will work, no food will be available and none can help. That will be the end of the pride of life in this world (Revelation 18:8).

This hunger is not always for physical food. There will be a famine of the hearing of the Word of God, of the revelation of Christ in the pulpit (Amos 8:11-14). Faith comes by hearing but in those days, there will be no real preaching that will glorify Christ and impart faith to the people. Many churches will die of spiritual hunger; they may have a sign outside but like a cemetery, there is no growth, no victory and no life inside (Revelation 3:1). Christ came to give us life abundantly (John 10:10). His plan is to seek and save that which was lost (Luke 19:10). At last, we shall stand around His Throne and worship Him freely; no more hunger, no more thirst, no more death. Our crowns at His feet, we shall behold Christ glorified forever (Revelation 7:13-17)! Amen!

OUR BREAD

In the King James Version of the Bible the word 'bread' appears 361 times. In other words, a loaf of bread is promised and given for each day of the year! To me this is a wonderful revelation! Bread is one of the oldest forms of food for man. God cursed the ground because of sin. Adam and his descendants will suffer before they can feed; they had to experience 'painful toil' before bread was placed on the table (Genesis 3:17-19). The work of the farmer is not easy. He has to trust God for the seed, for the rain, for the strength to labor and at last, for the harvest.

The process to make a loaf of bread is long and painful. We usually take the food for granted. Man takes pride in being self-made and the provider for food for the family. But the truth is that the Lord God gives food to His creation. From the mighty elephant, to the little sparrow; no one feeds by itself and no one sleeps hungry at night.

God gave his people bread in the wilderness for forty years. It was not the usual bread made from cereals. It was totally different; the people called it 'manna.' In Hebrew manna means 'what is that?' Something like flakes will be deposited on the ground early in the morning. The deposit of manna came with instructions to test the peoples' obedience. God chose 'the menu.' God chose 'the table manners.' They had to obey God who supplied the bread or they would suffer the consequences. There was no other food in the desert so the people had to humble themselves and obey God's commands. We see that the giving of Bread to satisfy hunger is connected with the difficult process of learning discipline.

There is a female character in the Bible called 'Madame Folly.' She is 'loud and undisciplined.' She calls and welcomes foolish people like herself, offering them stolen 'sweet' bread to eat (Proverbs 9:13-18). Her house is 'a den of robbers' (Jeremiah 7:11) where religious people flatter one another, provoking God with much deception. There is 'food' on the table but also quarrels and division (1Corinthians 11:17-220). There is the entertainment of the false gospel of self. In the house of Folly true worship and prayer is forbidden and God is not invited. Be warned! Sin is 'delicious' but it is sugar coated poison. Many discover the truth too late.

Don't forget: Bread on the table is a gift from the same God who sent His only Son to die for us that we may live. This is called the true Gospel of the Kingdom, the good news, the only hope for sinners and the narrow gate to eternal life. Bread on the table is a sign of God's mercy, forgiveness, and reconciliation with His people after a time of rebellion. During the time of Judges, the people disobeyed God and 'everyone did as he saw fit' (Judges 21:25). Many people, like Elimelech and his family, they were scattered because of the famine in the land. Naomi suffered a lot; her husband and sons got sick and died aboard. But this is the good news: "She heard in the country of Moab that the Lord had visited His people by giving them bread" (Ruth 1:6, NKJ). She and Ruth came to Bethlehem, whose name really means 'The House of Bread.' Here Ruth marries Boaz, her Kinsman Redeemer.

The lesson is simple: my greatest need is to know God as my Father. He will then feed me with bread. I should never desire food or pleasure if God is not 'in it.' If you obey God's Word you will live! If you rebel against God's Word you will die! Just bread alone cannot satisfy and cannot give or sustain life! You need God! You need Jesus!

Jesus resisted the devil in the wilderness. After forty days of fasting, He was hungry.
The devil tempted Him to make bread for Himself, from stones. He wanted Jesus to go ahead and eat, without praying to God for bread. The purpose of temptation was to produce rebellion in the Son of God. The Lord rejected him declaring that it is God's word of provision that will sustain Him always, in times of hunger or not.

Jesus is our True and Eternal Kinsman Redeemer. In His house there is Bread always because He is the Bread of life. When we pray to our Father in heaven: 'Give us today our daily bread…" we should not forget that the prayer is not just about physical hunger. First of all it is about our spiritual needs. Jesus told the crowd following Him; "I am the bread of life. He who comes to me will never go hungry and he who believes in me will never be thirsty" (John 6:35). Most of them desired only natural bread; their hearts were hardened by the sin of unbelief. They rejected Him and went away; hungry in their soul but too proud to believe. This is the call: come and eat "… the food that endures to eternal life which the Son of Man will give you" (Mark 6:52; John 6:27, 60).

Hunger is a sign of life. Dead people are not hungry; they do not need bread. Are you hungry for the Living God? Are you hungry for the Bread of life? Are you grateful for the provision of food on the table? Do you pray before you eat? May I never take God and His provision for granted! Never! In Jesus name, amen!

Forgive us our debts,
as we also have forgiven our debtors

"Forgive our debts, as we also have forgiven our debtors…"
~Matthew 6:12

PRAYER FOR PARDON

There are three requests in the Lord's Prayer: for provision, for pardon and for protection. We shall now study the second one, looking at the great need and the blessing of forgiveness.

Amongst the three personal requests, forgiveness is the only one that has an explanation attached to it at the end of the prayer: "For if you forgive men when they sin against you, your heavenly Father will also forgive you, but if you do not forgive men their sins, your Father will not forgive your sins' (Matthew 6:14, 15).

FORGIVENESS-definition:
Forgiveness means to let go, to loose, to give up the claim 'to host' three things:

- Anger (grudges, bitterness) coming from a hurt, an offense or a trespass against you by another,
- Wickedness: the lust for revenge (the desire to see the other suffer and be punished for hurting you),
- Greed (the desire to gain money as restitution from the one who cheated you).

Forgiveness is a choice and it is also 'a heart thing.' It is also a spiritual victory. By letting go of your rights to be angry, to see revenge and to become rich from another's suffering that means you chose the royal option of forgiveness. You bring your enemy and set him free at the foot of the cross. By doing this, you set yourself free from the burden of being the judge of the earth, an honor left for God alone.

FORGIVE US
Forgiveness is vertical first of all, then horizontal. We repent and pray to God for the forgiveness of sins. God is a God of justice. He forgives us because Jesus died on the Cross on our behalf. This is how we

89

have peace with God. This is vertical forgiveness and the root from where we receive the strength to forgive other men. You can only give to others from what God has deposited in you. You can only extend mercy and peace from the deposit of mercy and peace received at the Throne of the Lamb. We are FORGIVEN SO THAT WE MAY FORGIVE!

Just like the request for bread, we ask for forgiveness as a family. It is 'forgive us' not 'forgive me.' It is a prayer of intercession and the desire to spread the grace of compassion to as many that hear our prayers and connect with us. The source of forgiveness is God. It produces a great harvest of mercy in our hearts and an overflow of kindness to our enemies that will eventually conquer the evil around (Romans 12:17-21).

Forgiveness is very difficult, very costly. The desire for revenge is natural in a sinner's heart; to forgive is unnatural. Forgiveness is a supernatural decision done in the presence of God for the sake of Christ alone. It is a choice, the conscious act of the will. The feeling may betray you initially. When hurt, you may not feel any desire to forgive your enemy. You may struggle in your heart with feelings of vengeance and anger, but you can overrule them by the power of the will, strengthened by the Holy Spirit. That is why I said that you cannot truly forgive another, except you are truly saved.

The reason why it is so difficult to forgive is because showing mercy looks like weakness; it looks like the reaction of a loser. To exhibit anger, to warn others with vengeance… that looks like a champion's way of life. No one wants to be seen weak or as a coward. That is why only the children of God can forgive and win the battle against the strong, through the weakness and foolishness of the Cross, the mystery of God revealed to them alone.

Forgiveness is a command of Jesus and we want to obey it. We forgive because we have been forgiven by Jesus and we want to be like Him. This is the root of forgiveness. Only the truly saved understand the power of sin. They alone come to the Cross and have the burden and shame of sin forgiven. They know that Christ died in their place to pay the price for the forgiveness of their sins. The knowledge and understanding of the Cross will never depart from one who is truly saved. This knowledge of their identity in Christ helps them in the process of forgiveness.

When someone hurts you, offends you through words or actions, remember that sinners did much worst to your Lord. Remember that His last words when dying on the cross was a prayer of forgiveness for them that nailed Him there: "Father, forgive them for they do not know what they are doing" (Luke 23:34).

The message is simple: forgiveness is a test of life. They that know Christ and their identity in Him, they are the ones able to accommodate offense from others and to forgive them. Their forgiveness is a proof of their eternal life. They who are ignorant of Christ and of their identity in Him will be offended and they will not be able to forgive their enemies, but they will pursue them in vengeance even unto death.

AS WE FORGIVE OTHERS...

There are many scriptures that command us to choose love, mercy and forgiveness in our relationships with our people in general and with the brethren in particular. That is 'horizontal' forgiveness. To understand better, we shall study the 'parable of the unmerciful servant' in chapter eighteen of the book of Matthew.

There is a King who calls His servants to settle accounts with them. One of them owes Him ten thousand talents. This is a lot of money; a debt of almost twenty million dollars.

The man 'fell on his knees' and begged the King to have patience, that he will repay the debt. Because of his attitude of apparent humble worship, the King takes pity on him, cancels the debt and lets him go free. But when the servant goes out and meets another man who owes him a few dollars, he grabs and chokes him insisting on his money. The poor man begs in the same way as he did with the King, but he refuses to listen and throws him into debtors' prison until he pays back all of his debt. The other servants were 'distressed' and reported it to the King who became very angry with the 'wicked servant.'

He said that the mercy received from him should extend to others as a sign of appreciation and respect for Him who forgave freely. He then did what He wanted to do at the beginning and sent the unmerciful servant to prison where he will be tortured until he pays back all he owes. Jesus ends the parable with this warning: "This is how my heavenly Father will treat each of you unless you forgive your brother from your heart" (Matthew 17:35).

What is the lesson for us? We see here forgiveness as a test. It is only for the children of God who truly appreciate forgiveness! The King who settles the accounts with His servants is Jesus. He died for sinners to save them from the debt of sin and death. The Gospel of Christ is the good news of mercy, and grace, and freedom. We have to repent, believe in

Jesus, and become born again. We then become new creatures saved to produce fruit for His glory. We shall furthermore do good works that represent and honor Him. There is a danger to take His grace and mercy for granted. We may come to church, 'serve' God but we dishonor Him through the wrong attitudes of the heart. We keep grudges, anger, wickedness, envy, and hatred in the heart refusing to extend the grace we have experienced. That is false confidence, it grieves the Holy Spirit and it is a most dangerous path leading to untold suffering. To take God's grace for granted is to crucify Christ a second time. May God forbid such evil in our midst!

HOW DO WE KNOW THAT WE HAVE NOT TRULY FORGIVEN OTHERS? FEAR, GUILT, AND CONFUSSION

We said that forgiveness is a test. They that receive it and extend it to others are truly saved. The ones who take it for granted are not saved. They are religious hypocrites that failed the test of grace. They shall live in fear of punishment; their lives will be 'a living hell'; no hope for tomorrow. They experience 'torture and torment in prison.'

The word torment is defined as extremely painful, stressful, persistent attacks on the body and mind. It creates a constant state of anxiety, of fear, of danger; there is a feeling that death is coming close enough that you can touch it. You feel persecuted, mocked, intimidated and disgraced daily. You wish to die, but death does not come. It is a spiritual emergency of feeling oppressed and choked, that you can't breathe. Life becomes a struggle, like a drowning man alone in the sea; no friend, no light, nothing to hold. In other words, God will come to the unmerciful, unforgiving religious people and will destroy their false assurance that He has forgiven them in the past. There is no prayer that will be accepted except they come to the cross, humble themselves and repent. They have to surrender their lives to Christ, this time with all their heart, unconditionally.

In the Book of Luke chapter sixteen we see the rich man who died unrepentant, now in the torment of hell. He is thirsty and lacks any comfort. From there he sees poor Lazarus, who was once begging by his gate. The difference in their status is so great, and this adds to his torment. Then 'he looks up' and cries to Abraham for mercy, like the prayer of a desperate, dying man. But this is an impossible request. Prayers in hell cannot be answered. Mercy does not extend its ministry to the place where "...the worm does not die and the fire is not quenched" (Mark 9:48). Prayer for mercy and forgiveness is done on earth, to God and not to Abraham or any of the saints. It is done while there is time: 'Forgive us our sins as we forgive others...'

This is a warning to all religious people! God will allow this terrible torment so that for the first time in your life you'll see the need and the value of the Savior. You will learn the greatest lessons of all: that Jesus Christ is Lord of all!

HOW DO WE KNOW THAT WE HAVE TRULY FOR-GIVEN OTHERS?
PEACE AND FREEDOM

The opposite of the word torment is comfort, peace, security, deliverance and salvation. We know that we have truly forgiven others when we receive peace with God. The second sign is the power to love others freely. This is a clear sign that we are now born again (Romans 5:1-5; 1 John 3:11-24).

When we 'forgive others who trespass against us' we let go of the desire to see with our own eyes the punishment of the wicked. We are satisfied that God will do it in His own way and in His own time. We trust God for final justice. Forgiveness is a matter of faith in God! Let your faith increase to accommodate forgiveness!

It is a great blessing and great gain to know that you have passed the golden test of forgiveness. By letting go of grudges and anger, of bitterness, wickedness and greed, we shall experience freedom and peace with God and man. The difference is so clear, so great, that anyone who has experienced it will never be the same again. Pride dies instantly. Strongholds are destroyed. Humility and patience will be the mark upon the forgiven child of God. There is no fear of future torment for the merciful man who has been sealed with the Holy Spirit (Revelation 9). Out of the overflow of his heart, he will extend mercy to others as a point of contact with the Savior Jesus Christ. His ministry will be marked by love, wisdom, and anointing. He will be able to impact all nations with the power of the Cross. He will preach the True Gospel of free grace, lifting up

Christ Crucified. His desire will be to give glory to God and to live in the likeness of Christ. O, the power of such a life!

And lead us not into temptation
but deliver us from the evil one

"And lead us not into temptation but deliver us from the evil one"
~Matthew 6: 13

PRAYER OF PROTECTION

There is a need to pray for protection from the attacks of the devil, called the 'evil one.' The word 'protection' means to cover, to shield another who is smaller or weaker; to defend him from damage, hurt, or destruction. The Lord reminds us of the existence of the devil and the need for spiritual warfare.

Looking at the pattern of this prayer we see that it becomes more and more difficult. Each line challenges us to be involved personally and to participate actively, with faith and courage. The easiest, it seems, is the first line commanding us to 'hallow' God's name. Worship is not easy but it feels so because often we feel detached because of the distance between heaven and earth. The next line is more difficult, asking God to bring His will and kingdom to earth. The reason for the difficulty is that we see God's will 'coming down' to earth, closer to us. We cannot pray like this and be passive anymore.

Then we petition for bread. That is hard because we feel too proud for such a request. Then we pray for forgiveness, harder still because it is a matter of the heart and it exposes hidden sins. Lastly, we are to pray for protection from the 'evil one.' This is the hardest because we tend to ignore the reality of the devil and we assume that all we need is to worship God and make some requests. There are two parts to the above line of prayer: one is prevention and the second is for help during temptation.

1. Prevention of Temptation

It may seem strange to pray to God: 'Lead us not into temptation...' knowing that God does not tempt anyone to fall into sin.

"When tempted, no one should say "God is tempting me.' For God cannot be tempted by evil, nor does he tempt anyone; but each one is tempted when by his own evil desire he is dragged away and enticed. Then after the desire has conceived it gives birth to sin; and sin, when it is full grown, gives birth to death" (James 1:13-15).

Temptation is to attract by deception, by stirring the emotions, into a wrong path of sin, far from truth and safety. In the above verse we see the unholy chain of bondage that the devil uses to capture his unsuspecting victims. The beginning of the fall and failure that is to stir 'the evil desires'; weakness of his unsanctified heart. That is why we are commanded to be holy, to carry the cross daily; to die to sin and to the world and so destroy the point of contact for the devil. 'Prevention is better than cure.' To have a pure, holy heart is great gain and the foundation of victory against all temptation.

God is 'in a class of His own' when it comes to temptation: God cannot sin during any temptation by the devil. That is why our duty is to be like Jesus, victorious over temptation through faith in the Word of God.

The devil has a plan, a strategy to attract, to deceive, to draw away from safety, to capture the believer when he is weak and to bring him back into slavery of sin. It is a process that involves the senses, the body, the mind and the imagination. Each step brings the victim closer to the bondage of sin and death. We are commanded: "Do not let sin reign in your mortal body so that you obey its evil desires... but rather offer yourselves to God... for sin shall not be our master..." (Romans 6:12-14).

Sin is defined like a person who loves you and wants to 'marry you'; to rule over you like a king or master. Sin has a sweet voice of flattery to impress you with its 'freedom' and adventure. Sin will tell you that holiness is boring. There is temptation and deception behind all 'the pleasures of sin.' For example, Moses passed the test, but Cain failed (Hebrews 11:25; Genesis 4:6-8).

THE TESTS OF GOD

The power of sin and evil competes with God's Word in the fight to control your heart. The victory or the failure is first of all in your spirit. The devil wants to be worshipped. He hates you as you worship God. It is a war of romance and love, life and death. 'God does not tempt anyone.' He leads none into sin. God is holy and He hates sin. This is the truth revealed in His Word.

95

God is jealous over you. From time to time He allows the devil to come and tempt you. It is called the test of God, to prove if you are faithful to Him or if you take His love for granted. He wants you to remain actively faithful to Him, always. Great lesson: God does not tempt but He tests the hearts of His children. A sanctified heart is prepared for the tests of God!

"If a prophet or one who foretells by dreams appears among you and announces to you a miraculous sign or wonder and if the sign or wonder of which he has spoken takes place and he says: "Let us follow other gods (gods you have not known) and let us worship them, you must not listen to the words of that prophet or dreamer. The Lord your God is testing you to find out whether you love him with all your heart and with all your soul" (Deuteronomy 13:1-3).

This is a clear message that God wants us to love Him with all our heart. That is why He allows testing to come: to purify the motives. The devil will tempt us with his fake love. He wants to steal our heart from worshipping God. The devil covets worship. He was ready to give up the whole world for a moment of worship from the Son of God (Matthew 4:8-10). Be ready to reject the devil through the Word of God and prayer!

OBEDIENCE IS SAFETY

There is another spiritual principle we see in the Bible. God gives us His Word, His commands. We are to choose obedience and reject rebellion. This choice to be faithful and obedient is the foundation of our surrender to Christ. But the same choice is reinforced daily, each time truth is presented to us. A life of diligent obedience is a life of faith, of holiness, and blessings follow automatically, according to God's promise. This is called the 'Way of the Cross,' the narrow, royal way of spiritual maturity and it leads to eternal life. God's presence is assured and constant. Jesus said: "I will never leave you, nor forsake you…" God teaches and tests us by His very presence that never departs, encouraging us to move ahead.

DISOBEDIENCE LEADS INTO TEMPTATION AND SIN

But there is another option and unfortunately, many are misled into its easy slippery grounds. It is possible that you have 'accepted' Christ and you agree in general with the principle of obedience and faith. You may even preach about it. But when it comes to the practical application of it in daily life, especially when things are hard to obey, you 'draw back' doubting God and rebel. If you are indeed a child of God, you'll imme- diately sense the loss of peace. This is because you have grieved the Holy Spirit. This anxiety is an emergency signal that you should stop at once, repent and come back to the safety of the Cross. If you insist in rebellion, ignoring all the signals of jealous love from the Father, then you will have to be chastised by Him. The process is very painful and it is called 'lead- ing into temptation.' That is why we pray to the Father that we may not have to go there. During this time of chastisement, the Father will allow the devil to do the ugly work, to tempt, to vex, and to trouble. The com- forting presence of God will leave you, as it was with Samson. You will be abandoned for a season to the chains of bondage and hard labor. As a backslider, you will lose the joy of your salvation, your rewards and crowns. 'Father, have mercy…' we see that Jesus is teaching us to desire with all our heart to love the Father and to be faithful to Him always. He is telling us that we should be aware of the danger of rebellion and de- ception in the heart, that we should not trust ourselves but God with the deeper work of sanctification inside. We should gladly choose God's test than to go astray and be deceived by the devil's cheap 'love.' David was 'a man after God's heart.' After being tempted by the devil to be proud because of his great army, he quickly repented and chose God's punish- ment because of His mercy in judgment.

"Then David said to God; I have sinned greatly… This is what the Lord says: I am giving you three options. Choose one of them for me to carry out against you… David said …I am in deep distress… let me fall into the hands of the Lord for his mercy is very great; but do not let me fall into the hands of men" (1Chronicles 21:1-13).

The same principal appears in other scriptures. Simply said, God's way of the Cross or men's ways incited by the devil (Psalm 106:13-15; Romans 1:18-32). Anyone who chooses to be 'led into temptation,' into the domain of the devil, thinking it is an easier way, that man becomes a hindrance to Jesus and a stumbling block to the increase of His Kingdom on earth. Jesus called Peter 'Satan' and rebuked him for ignorance and deception. That is a terrible warning indeed (Matthew 16:23). God's test- ing is our gain. Rejoice during the test! This is how we learn patience, character, and maturity. We should rejoice when we sense God's pres- ence in the midst of the storm. It is a great privilege to have Jesus 'sleep- ing in your boat' as the winds and waves of oppression attack you on every side. The increase of patience in your heart is sure proof that God is in charge of the process of testing. It will lead to hope that is totally supernatural, for the glory of God (Romans 5:1-5; James 1:1-5).

Meditate on the Master's promise: "Since you have kept my command to endure patiently I will also keep you from the hour of trial that is going to come upon the whole world to test those who live on the earth" (Revelation 3:10). The words trial and test here are better understood as 'temptation."

2. Deliverance from Temptation
"No temptation has seized you except what is common to man. And God is faithful; he will not let you be tempted beyond what you can bear. But when you are tempted he will also provide a way out so that you can stand under it" (1 Corinthians 10:13).

The above promise has been a source of comfort to millions of believers. We are told that God knows our weakness. He gives us strength to endure during seasons of trials. He will never allow us to be broken beyond repair. As it was with Job, God limits and controls the damage of the devil and ultimately changes the story. God is faithful in His ways. "When we are tempted,' that means during the very pain of trial, Jesus reveals Himself as 'the Door of Escape,' a supernatural revelation of going out of the heat of the furnace. Like the spies went down from the window of Rehab at Jericho, by the scarlet cord of freedom, the way of escape is supernatural and easy. As the trial is difficult and raging, so the freedom is easy and sweet.

In conclusion: Obey the command of Jesus; "Watch and pray that you will not fall into temptation…" (Mark 14:38).

Let's pray:

Father I am ready to obey Your Word and cooperate with Your Spirit to change my heart until it is pure, holy, faithful, and true in worshipping you. Please, teach me and test me until I become acceptable in your sight as a holy vessel made fit for your use alone. You are good and merciful. I refuse to be stubborn and rebellious. I refuse to be led into temptation and to be taught by the devil in the hard way. I want to learn the very lesson you desire to teach me. Dear Father, I don't trust myself for my heart is deceitful. But I trust you alone to make my path straight in your presence. I refuse to move in the crooked, dark, and dangerous alleys of sin. Holy Spirit be my teacher! Lead me into the whole truth and show me things to come that I may be prudent in detecting deception and flee from sin at all costs.

I worship you Father for there is none who can answer this request for pure worship except you. In Jesus' name I pray, amen!

For Thine is the Kingdom and the Power and the Glory, Forever, Amen.

"For thine is the kingdom and the power and the glory, forever. Amen"
~Matthew 6:13 KJ

This is the last line of the Lord's Prayer. We started with worship; we end with praise. True prayer is inspired by the Holy Spirit, it touches the heart and lips of the believers, then goes back to heaven to our High Priest who faithfully 'collects' it. At last, mature prayer arrives at the Father where the real chemistry happens: prayer and its answer becomes glory to God.

'THINE IS THE KINGDOM'- FOREVER!

The scripture above starts with the word 'for.' I am reminded that the reason my prayer 'works' is because in Christ I belong to the eternal Kingdom of Heaven. Just in case I need to be reminded, here I see that my prayer spoken in the name of Jesus can never die. Even if I forget, God does not forget it. The Kingdom endures and expands forever. His Power works forever. His Glory shines forever. My prayer brings me into a realm where death has no words to offend and no tools to destroy. The visible answer to my prayers may come after my lifetime on earth has ended. I may be in heaven among the clouds of witnesses and worshippers, looking down on earth. But I will surely rejoice with the effect of my prayers on earth. The eternal value of prayers should encourage me to pray more, and better, and bigger. The word 'forever' should become part of my vocabulary. When I talk to a man, even if he is a king on this earth, I have to be careful with my words; let them not be too many or too direct. I have to remind myself of the human protocol. Let my imagination not run 'too wild. I may be shy to express my dreams to men, but oh... it is not so with God! Most of the time our prayers are too shallow; our requests too limited; our aim too low.

Our Lord encourages us to think having eternity in mind. My heart and my prayers should not see death as the end of my life. This is a strange thing for us, little people with little desires. It takes a long time to learn how to soar spiritually. Flying like an eagle is not a skill we desire to practice. But this is the secret; this is how we find our identity in Christ and this is how we fulfill our eternal destiny in Him.

A priest is called to pray and intercede. We are a 'royal priesthood' called to declare praises to God (1 Peter 2:9). There is an acceptable sacrifice of praise that pleases God (Hebrews 13:15). A sacrifice means death. In the past, an animal without blemish was brought to the altar to be slain there. The blood was shed for the forgiveness of sin of the one who offered it.

To offer sacrifice of praise means that we die to self, to our natural desires and will. Our feelings have to be offered on the altar before our mouth can offer sacrificial praise. It is easy to pray when all things look good. It is hard when things are difficult. But we continue to pray and praise God even when we don't feel like it; even when talking to God feels like such an added burden. We have to make a choice to maintain 'the line of prayer open' to God, to pray 'always' and 'without ceasing.' That is called a sacrifice acceptable to God. It is not just acceptable, but it is peculiar, unique. The saints in heaven do not praise God as a sacrifice. It is never 'hard' for them to talk to God because there is no hindrance and no opposition. They don't need faith to pray because they see Jesus face to face always and they worship Him freely. But here on earth, it is hard, it is by faith, it is a sacrifice. And yes, it is pleasing to our Father in heaven.

Oh, that we may continue to talk to God even when there is no apparent answer, for he that promised is faithful!

The Lord is teaching us that He will hear and answer the prayer. We shall not be ashamed of our prayers. He will answer and we shall rejoice, praising Him forever.

That is the foundation of the Kingdom of God. You should never doubt that God is interested in every detail of your life. Never lose your hope in the God who invented prayer!

'THINE IS THE POWER'– FOREVER!

'Power belongs to God' (Psalm 62:11). His power is not like a hurricane that destroys all in its path. God's power is selective and accurate. God never makes mistakes. He destroys all barriers and strongholds of the evil ones and by the same power He sets the captives free. God does not destroy the victims. When Jericho fell, with all the terrible sound and shaking surrounding it, Rehab and her family were saved. God's power has the final say in all events. None can stop it.

Remember as you are praying: the God we serve, our Heavenly Father, He is all powerful. Never forget that! The devil may tempt you that some things are too difficult for God to do. That is a lie that produces doubt, a strong hindrance to continue the prayer. Many people fail the test of faith. Oh, that we may desire to know God's power, not just in doctrine but in experience. If you are tempted to think that all this talk about the cross and resurrection is just history, that it only applies to Jesus and not to you, that is another lie. Many people go to church and pray often, but they doubt this power that has the last say in all human affairs. For me, just memorizing some scriptures about the power of God has been of great help during prayer. Then my faith rises and I touch the Throne of God. I enter with worship, I continue with prayer and I end up in praise to God!

"Praise be to you, O Lord… from everlasting to everlasting. Yours, O Lord, is the greatness and the power and the glory and the majesty and the splendor, for everything in heaven and earth is yours. Yours, O Lord, is the Kingdom… Now, our Lord, we give thanks and praise your glorious name" (1 Chronicles 29:10-13).

I believe that God is happy when we pray with passion and courage, with boldness and confidence, soaring above the low, dark clouds of doubt and fear. Like a champion, I do not compete with others in the spiritual exercise of prayer, but I challenge myself and improve my own record. I pray louder and longer. I pray even when I don't know what to pray. I pray in the Spirit when my human language fails. To some people, it may look like a joke but to me it is true prayer and I know that it will not be in vain. I soak my life and ministry with a flood of prayers. I never regret it. It is a good and blessed habit that yields much fruit.

'THINE IS THE GLORY'- FOREVER!

This praise chorus that ends the Lord's Prayer tells me that I should desire that all my petitions and requests should give God all the glory. I believe that God 'edits' our prayers in such a way that the answer will give Him the glory. This is a very important lesson that we should never forget. We pray for provision, we intercede for others, we pray for healing and victory in warfare. But we should pray for wisdom to know what pleases God and what give Him glory. The more we understand that, the more confidence we have in prayer and the faster the answer will come. That is to have the mind of Christ, to be spiritually mature and fruitful, worshipping God with prayers that supply heaven with incense for more worship to the glory of His name.

"...they were holding golden bowls full of incense which are the prayers of the saints... In a loud voice they sang: Worthy is the Lamb who was slain to receive power and wealth and wisdom and strength and honor and glory and praise...forever and ever!" (Revelation 5:8-13).

AND THEN I PRAYED!

"Dear God, if you exist, then come down from heaven and change my heart. I am tired of doubting you. I can't wait forever for the answer to this prayer. I will give you one month's notice to come down from heaven and change my heart. If you come, I promise to be your friend forever. In Jesus name I pray, amen!"

I did not know the meaning of the name Jesus, but I heard people pray like that, so I guessed it was an appropriate end to a prayer. Immediately, I knew that something 'good' had happened to me. Not certain of what, but the sense of destiny came down and enveloped my soul. I felt life entering my veins. In exactly twenty eight days the Spirit of God came down on me and filled my soul. I became a child of God.

Today, this prayer sounds so childish, so simple. But even now, after so many years, I can still say that it was a real prayer from a broken heart that God did not despise. Each time I am tempted to be proud, because of some achievements in church, or because of added gifts and wisdom, I look back at the beginning, at the time when I placed all on the altar and died to myself.

My first prayer was an accepted sacrifice. God heard me and answered with peace and joy beyond words to describe. This is my foundation as a believer. He taught me how to pray and worship. He collected my tears so that none would be wasted. He loved me first until my heart responded to the strings of His passion.

Dear reader, please believe that God is faithful and real. Please believe that He is our God forever. He is our Friend and Bridegroom, and one day we shall see Him face to face. May He find us spotless and pure! May He rejoice in the work of His hands in our lives! May Jesus Christ be glorified in all of us forever! Let us bow and thank our Father for the privilege of prayer.

"Lord, I am forever grateful. Amen"!

www.ingramcontent.com/pod-product-compliance
Lightning Source LLC
Chambersburg PA
CBHW031518040426

42445CB00009B/284